THE PARADOXES OF LEGAL SCIENCE

THE PARADOXES OF
LEGAL SCIENCE

By

BENJAMIN N. CARDOZO

GREENWOOD PRESS, PUBLISHERS
WESTPORT, CONNECTICUT

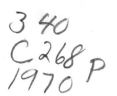

CONTENTS

PAGE

I

INTRODUCTION — REST AND MOTION — STABILITY
AND PROGRESS 1

II

THE MEANING OF JUSTICE — THE SCIENCE OF
VALUES 31

III

THE EQUILIBRATION OF INTERESTS — CAUSE AND
EFFECT — THE INDIVIDUAL AND SOCIETY —
LIBERTY AND GOVERNMENT 67

IV

LIBERTY AND GOVERNMENT — CONCLUSION . . 102

INDEX 137

v

I

INTRODUCTION — REST AND MOTION — STABILITY AND PROGRESS

"They do things better with logarithms." The wail escapes me now and again when after putting forth the best that is in me, I look upon the finished product, and cannot say that it is good. In these moments of disquietude, I figure to myself the peace of mind that must come, let us say, to the designer of a mighty bridge. The finished product of his work is there before his eyes with all the beauty and simplicity and inevitableness of truth. He is not harrowed by misgivings whether the towers and piers and cables will stand the stress and strain. His business is to know. If his bridge were to fall, he would go down with it in disgrace and ruin. Yet withal, he has never a fear. No mere experiment has he wrought, but a highway to carry men and women from shore to shore, to carry them secure and unafraid, though the floods rage and boil below.

So I cry out at times in rebellion, "why cannot I do as much, or at least something measurably as much, to bridge with my rules of law the torrents of life?" I have given my years to the task, and behind me are untold generations, the judges and lawgivers

1

of old, who strove with a passion as burning. Code
and commentary, manor-roll and year-book, treatise
and law-report, reveal the processes of trial and
error by which they struggled to attain the truth,
enshrine their blunders and their triumphs for warning and example. All these memorials are mine; yet
unwritten is my table of logarithms, the index of the
power to which a precedent must be raised to produce
the formula of justice. My bridges are experiments.
I cannot span the tiniest stream in a region unexplored by judges or lawgivers before me, and go to
rest in the secure belief that the span is wisely laid.

Let me not seem to cavil at the difficulties that
learning can subdue. They are trying enough in all
conscience, yet what industry can master, it would
be weakness to lament. I am not thinking of the multitude of precedents and the labor of making them
our own. The pangs that convulse are born of other
trials. Diligence and memory and normal powers of
reasoning may suffice to guide us truly in those fields
where the judicial function is imitative or static,
where known rules are to be applied to combinations
of facts identical with present patterns, or, at worst,
but slightly different. The travail comes when the
judicial function is dynamic or creative. The rule
must be announced for a novel situation where com-
petitive analogies supply a hint or clew, but where
precedents are lacking with authoritative commands.

I know the common answer to these and like la-
ments. The law is not an exact science, we are told,

and there the matter ends, if we are willing there to
end it. One does not appease the rebellion of the intellect by the reaffirmance of the evil against which
intellect rebels. Exactness may be impossible, but
this is not enough to cause the mind to acquiesce in
a predestined incoherence. Jurisprudence will be the
gainer in the long run by fanning the fires of mental
insurrection instead of smothering them with plati-
tudes. "If science," says Whitehead,[1] "is not to de-
generate into a medley of *ad hoc* hypotheses, it
must become philosophical and must enter upon a
thorough criticism of its own foundations." We may
say the like of law.

So I keep reaching out and groping for a pathway
to the light. The outlet may not be found. At least
there may be glimmerings that will deny themselves
to a craven *non possumus,* the sterility of ignoble
ease. Somewhere beneath the welter, there may be a
rationalizing principle revealing system and harmony in what passes for discord and disorder. Modern science is tending to revolutionize our ideas of
motion within the atom, and so of motion generally.
We had thought of radiation as continuous and flow-
ing. We are told that in truth it is discrete and irregular.[2] The electron does not glide from point to
point. The goal is gained *per saltum.* "There is a
possibility that the old laws, which represented mo-

[1] *Science and the Modern World*, p. 24.
[2] Whitehead, *op. cit.*, pp. 50, 181; Bertrand Russell, *The A.B.C.
of Atoms*, pp. 9, 54, 55, and the same author's "Philosophy," pp.
101, 107.

tion as a continuous smooth process, may be only statistical averages, and that when we come down to a sufficiently minute scale, everything really proceeds by jumps, like the cinema, which produces a misleading appearance of continuous motion by means of a succession of separate pictures.''[3] Is it possible that in rationalizing the development of law, in measuring the radiating energy of principle and precedent, we have been hampered by a like illusion? We have sought for a formula consistent with steady advance through a continuum. The continuum does not exist. Instead there are leaps from point to point. We have been beguiled by the ideal of an harmonious progression. Centres of energy exist, of attraction and repulsion. A landing-place is found between them. We make these landing places for ourselves through the methods of the judicial process. How shall they be wrought? Where shall they be found?

The reconciliation of the irreconcilable, the merger of antitheses, the synthesis of opposites, these are the great problems of the law. ''Nomos,'' one might fairly say, is the child of antinomies, and is born of them in travail. We fancy ourselves to be dealing with some ultra-modern controversy, the product of the clash of interests in an industrial society. The problem is laid bare, and at its core are the ancient mysteries crying out for understanding — rest and motion, the one and the many, the self and the not-

[3] Bertrand Russell, *The A.B.C. of Atoms*, p. 9; *cf.* Bertrand Russell, ''Mathematics and Metaphysics,'' in *Mysticism and Logic*, p. 84.

self, freedom and necessity, reality and appearance,
the absolute and the relative. We have the claims of
stability to be harmonized with those of progress.
We are to reconcile liberty with equality, and both
of them with order. The property rights of the individual we are to respect, yet we are not to press them
to the point at which they threaten the welfare or the
security of the many. We must preserve to justice
its universal quality, and yet leave to it the capacity
to be individual and particular. The precedent or the
statute, though harsh, is to be obeyed, yet obeyed
also, at the sacrifice not seldom of the written word,
are to be the meliorating precepts of equity and conscience. Events are to be traced to causes, yet since
causes are infinite in number, there must be a process of selection by which the cause to be assigned as
operative will vary with the end in view. Is this
dreamland or reality? The ground seems to slip beneath our feet, yet a foothold must be found. "Fundamental opposites," I quote from a different context
the words of Lytton Strachey in his essay on Pope,
"fundamental opposites clash and are reconciled."
   The problem points the method. The goal of juridical effort, says Demogue, is not logical synthesis,
but compromise. "Of course," he adds, "this makes
the law a subtle science, but it cannot be avoided." [4]
A like bifurcation, the opposition between static and

[4] Demogue, *Analysis of Fundamental Notions*, vol. 7, Modern Legal
Philosophy Series, p. 570. *Cf.* Bryce, *Studies in History and Jurisprudence*, quoted by Andrews, "Recent Decisions of the Court of Appeals," 12 *Cornell Law Quarterly*, 433.

dynamic, divides the universe.[5] So at least it seems
to us today, though the truth of the division may be
one that is relative to our own imperfect minds, unable to penetrate to the unity in which diversity is
lost.[6] Until deeper insight is imparted to us, we must
be content with many a makeshift compromise, with
many a truth that is approximate and relative, when
we are yearning for the absolute. "To bring about
reconciliations," I quote Demogue again, "is the
great work of jurists."[7]

Let us summon a few of these antitheses before us
and watch the process of compromise as it mediates
between them. Rest competes with motion, perma-
nence with flux, stability with progress. Where shall
compromise draw the line? The "one" is in rivalry
with the "many," the individual with the group, the
group with the community, liberty with restraint.
Where is the line that we shall call the jural median?
"Perfect security," says Demogue,[8] "would mean
the infinite immobility of society," to which we add
that perfect certainty would mean the same. The
friends of constitutional government are prompt to
repel encroachments upon liberty, yet liberty in the
literal sense is desired only by the anarchists,[9] with
whom the friends of constitutional government

---

[5] Demogue, *op. cit.*, pp. 429, 430, 448.

[6] Haldane, *The Reign of Relativity*, pp. 11, 37, 63; Dewey, *Experience and Nature*, p. 46.

[7] Demogue, *op. cit.*, p. 570.

[8] *Op. cit.*, p. 445.

[9] G. Lowes Dickinson, *Justice and Liberty*, p. 142.

would scorn to claim accord. Deep beneath the surface of the legal system, hidden in the structure of the constituent atoms, are these attractions and repulsions, uniting and dissevering as in one unending paradox. "Fundamental opposites clash and are reconciled."

In my study of antinomies, I start with the antithesis between rest and motion, stability and progress. "There are two principles," says Whitehead,[10] "inherent in the very nature of things, recurring in some particular embodiments whatever field we explore — the spirit of change, and the spirit of conservation. There can be nothing real without both. Mere change without conservation is a passage from nothing to nothing. Its final integration yields mere transient non-entity. Mere conservation without change cannot conserve. For after all, there is a flux of circumstance, and the freshness of being evaporates under mere repetition." If life feels the tug of these opposing tendencies, so also must the law which is to prescribe the rule of life. We are told at times that change must be the work of statute, and that the function of the judicial process is one of conservation merely. But this is historically untrue, and were it true, would be unfortunate. Violent breaks with the past must come, indeed, from legislation, but manifold are the occasions when advance or retrogression is within the competence of judges as their competence has been determined by practice and tra-

[10] *Science and the Modern World*, p. 281.

dition. The law has its formulas, and its methods of judging, appropriate to conservation, and its methods and formulas appropriate to change. If we figure stability and progress as opposite poles, then at one pole we have the maxim of *stare decisis* and the method of decision by the tool of a deductive logic; at the other we have the method which subordinates origins to ends. The one emphasizes considerations of uniformity and symmetry, and follows fundamental conceptions to ultimate conclusions. The other gives freer play to considerations of equity and justice, and the value to society of the interests affected. The one searches for the analogy that is nearest in point of similarity, and adheres to it inflexibly. The other, in its choice of the analogy that shall govern, finds community of spirit more significant than resemblance in externals. "Much of the administration of justice," says Pound,[11] "is a compromise between the tendency to treat each case as one of a generalized type of case, and the tendency to treat each case as unique."[12] Each method has its value, and for each in the changes of litigation there will come the hour for use. A wise eclecticism employs them both. Often the motivating force behind a choice will seem to be nothing more rational than mere empirical opportunism. This does not mean that the study of the process of selection yields nothing of utility. We may hit upon uniformities that will

[11] Article "Jurisprudence" in the *History and Prospects of the Social Sciences*, by Harry Elmer, Barnes, and others, p. 472.
[12] *Cf.* Cardozo, *The Growth of the Law*, p. 67.

help us in the course of time to the formulation of a principle. If the generalizations of jurisprudence are imperfect and provisional, so also, at least in the early stages of development, are those of science everywhere. "The things directly observed," it has been said,[13] "are, almost always, only samples. We want to conclude that the abstract conditions which hold for the samples, also hold for all other entities which, for some reason or other, appear to us to be of the same sort. This process of reasoning from the sample to the whole species is Induction. The theory of Induction is the despair of philosophy — and yet all our activities are based upon it." The jurist must have the patience and the faith that have inspired the meditations of the physicist, and have crowned experiment with triumph.

At the outset, there is need to delimit the subject matter of our study. Our concern is with the law as it is shaped by the judicial process. Statutes may be put aside except in so far as they require the work of judges to expound them, for to the extent that their commands are unmistakable their interest is not so much for jurisprudence as for the science of legislation. I do not mean to suggest that the study of the process of legislation may not be fruitful of results. The truth is that many of us, bred in common law traditions, view statutes with a distrust which we may deplore, but not deny. This has led, as you know, to the maxim of construction that stat-

[13] Whitehead, *op. cit.*, p. 34.

utes derogating from the common law are to be
strictly construed, a maxim which recalls what has
been said by Sir Frederick Pollock of rules of statutory construction generally: they cannot well be
accounted for except on the theory that the legislature generally changes the law for the worse, and
that the business of judges is to keep the mischief of
its interference within the narrowest possible
bounds.[14] I do not forget a trenchant article by Roscoe Pound in which he exhibits this distrust as narrow minded in its origin and pernicious in its tendency.[15] I do not dwell upon his criticism now, for it is
foreign to my theme. Perhaps a scientific study of
legislation, its capacities and limitations, would
bring us to a saner attitude. The point I wish to
make is that our concern for the moment is with the
work of judges only, and with law as it issues from
their hands. So far as they are the mere mouthpiece
of a legislature, speaking thoughts and enforcing
commands that have been unmistakably set down,
their activity is in its essence administrative and not
judicial. Where doubt enters in, there enters the
judicial function.

I come back to the antithesis between rest and
motion. We live in a world of change. If a body of
law were in existence adequate for the civilization of
today, it could not meet the demands of the civilization of tomorrow. Society is inconstant. So long as

14 Pollock, *Essays in Jurisprudence and Ethics*, p. 85.
15 Pound, ''Common Law and Legislation,'' 21 *Harvard L. R.* 383.

it is inconstant, and to the extent of such inconstancy, there can be no constancy in law. The kinetic forces are too strong for us. We may think the law is the same if we refuse to change the formulas. The identity is verbal only. The formula has no longer the same correspondence with reality. Translated into conduct, it means something other than it did. Law defines a relation not always between fixed points, but often, indeed oftenest, between points of varying position. The acts and situations to be regulated, have a motion of their own. There is change whether we will it or not.[16]

One is reminded of the Einstein theory and the relativity of motion. "Stated generally, the teaching of Einstein is that absolute rest and motion are meaningless for physical science, and that motion can signify only the changing position of bodies relatively to each other."[17] If there were infinite space with only one object in it, motion for that object would have no meaning to our minds. If in infinite space there were only two objects, motion would still be without meaning so long as relatively to each other the positions were the same. There is need to import some of this same conception of relativity into our conception of the development of

16 *Cf.* M. R. Cohen, ''The Place of Logic in the Law,'' 29 *Harvard Law Review,* 629; Frankfurter, ''Hours of Labor and Realism,'' 29 *H. L. R.* 369.

17 Haldane, *The Reign of Relativity,* p. 55; *cf.* p. 92; Bertrand Russell, *The A. B. C. of Relativity,* pp. 24, 69.

law.[18] We render judgment by establishing a relation between moving objects — moving at different speeds and in different directions. If we fix the relation between them upon the assumption that they are stationary, the result will often be to exaggerate the distance. True constancy consists in fitting our statement of the relation to the new position of the objects and the new interval between them.

I find an illustration of my thought in the development of the law governing ocean bills of lading. One will see the history of the development well and graphically portrayed in an article in the *Yale Law Journal* by Mr. Chester B. McLaughlin, Jr., a member of the New York bar.[19] At first a bill of lading imported the delivery of merchandise on board a designated ship. The time came, however, with the upheavals of the Great War when the goings and comings of ships were too uncertain to be known or stated in advance. Goods were left at the dock, and all that the steamship company would undertake was to send them forward when it could. "During the war the whole routine of transoceanic shipments was destroyed, and no steamship company was able to predict even within months when it would be able to ship goods or on what steamer." [20] The documents issued to its shippers conformed to these necessities.

18 *Cf.* Lippmann, *The Phantom Public*, p. 89; W. F. Ogburn, *Social Change*, p. 199; Sorokin, *Social Mobility*, p. 4.

19 "The Evolution of the Ocean Bill of Lading," 35 *Yale Law Journal* 549.

20 McLaughlin, *supra*, p. 559.

They no longer acknowledged receipt on a designated vessel. The acknowledgment was merely that the goods had been received for shipment on a named vessel "and / or on a following steamer." When the war was over, the change that had thus been born of necessity was continued for convenience. "The necessities of proper stowage and the irregularity in arrival of shipments combined with the great accumulation of cargo, both inward and outward, on the piers and for different steamers" were thought to "render it physically impossible either to guarantee loading by a particular vessel, or to determine until after a steamer is loaded and the dock checked up whether any specific cargo had been loaded." [21] The old form of document thus came to be supplanted by a new one which omitted an acknowledgment once recognized as vital. The question was still open as to the extent to which the courts would effectuate the change. A bank was to pay for goods against a draft and a bill of lading. Was a document in the new form a bill of lading against which payment might be made? To have said "no" would have kept the law consistent with ancient definitions. To have said "yes" kept it consistent with the realities of usage and the needs of ocean commerce. In this dilemma, the courts preferred to answer "yes." [22] The truth, of course, was that there had been a change in methods of transportation which necessitated a revision

[21] McLaughlin, *supra,* p. 560.

[22] Vietor *v.* National City Bank, 200 App. Div. 557; 1923, 237 N.Y. 538.

of the legal formula if the relation defined by law was to maintain its former correspondence with the relation to be regulated, *i.e.*, the relation known to business. Refusal to change the statement of the rule would have given to the change of events an exaggerated movement. Revision of the legal formula by keeping it in pace with the movement of events preserved its correspondence with existing norms of conduct.

I find another illustration in the capacity of the law merchant to extend the quality of negotiability to novel forms of documents if negotiable by custom.[23] This capacity may, of course, be arrested by statute, as in New York and other states.[24] In the absence of such restraint, there are few tendencies of growth more persistent and effective. The parallelism is maintained between the movement of legal concepts and that of mercantile expedients.

From these and kindred illustrations a working rule emerges. In default of a better name, I may style it the principle of relativity in the adaptation of the law to conduct. When changes of manners or business have brought it about that a rule of law which corresponded to previously existing norms or standards of behavior, corresponds no longer to the present norms or standards, but on the contrary departs from them, then those same forces or tend-

[23] See, *e.g.*, Goodwin *v.* Robarts, *L. R.*, 10 Ex. 346; Bechuan Land Exploration Co. *v.* London Trading Co., 1898, 2 Q.B. 658; Edelstein *v.* Schuler, 1902, 2 K.B. 144, 154.

[24] Bank of Manhattan Company *v.* Morgan, 1926, 242 N.Y. 38.

encies of development that brought the law into
adaptation to the old norms and standards are effective, without legislation, but by the inherent energies of the judicial process, to restore the equilibrium.
In formulating this canon I do not mean that it is
capable of slavish application. No rule of thumb will
tell us in advance when events in their movement
have traversed such a distance that to avoid undue
disparity we must reformulate the rule of law. Many
factors of convenience must be counted. Many observations from different angles must be made before the survey will be accurate. Then, when dis-
tances have been measured, the canon may be borne
in mind. Precedent or formal logic may seem to be
pointing to stability. The principle of relativity in
the adaptation of the law to conduct may point the
way to change.
My illustrations have been drawn from changing
forms of business. What is true of motion there is
true, and for like reasons, of motion in the realm of
morals. Manners and customs (if we may not label
them as law itself) are at least a source of law. The
judge, so far as freedom of choice is given to him,
tends to a result that attaches legal obligation to the
folkways, the norms or standards of behavior exem-
plified in the life about him.[25] Manners and customs
are equally a source of morals. One has only to

25 Willis, J., in Millar *v.* Taylor, 1769, 4 Burr. 2303, 2312, quoted
by Lefroy, 32 *L.Q.R.* 294.

glance at such a book as Sumner's *Folkways* or Hobhouse's *Morals in Evolution* to have this truth brought home with superabundant demonstration. Not that morals in our own day are compact of custom and nothing else. Undoubtedly, as Hobhouse has well brought out, reflection has combined with imitation, reasoning with mere mechanical repetition, philosophy with tradition, in the forming of the compound.[26] ''As we follow the ethical movement in its advance, we shall find more and more that the interest shifts from the tradition which men follow half mechanically to the deliberate attempt to reorganize conduct on the basis of some distinct theory of life.''[27] ''In ethics, custom and theory are in constant and close interaction, and our subject, the comparative study of ethics, must embrace them both. It would include, were it within one man's power to treat it exhaustively, at one extreme the quasi-instinctive judgment based on the unthinking acceptance of tradition; at the other the profoundest theory of the thinker seeking a rational basis of conduct and an intelligible formula to express the end of life, and between these two the influences, rational and half rational, which are at work with increasing assiduity as civilization advances, remodelling custom and substituting deliberately accepted principle, whether

[26] *Cf.* MacIver, *Community*, pp. 149, 150; Vinogradoff, *Custom and Right*, p. 34; ''A comparative survey of western European customs discloses, as it seems to me, three main factors: business practice, tradition, and reflective formulation.'' — Vinogradoff, *op. cit.*

[27] Hobhouse, *Morals in Evolution*, p. 18.

true, half true or false, for blind tradition.''[28] ''Our
subject must include the ideal of the apostle as well
as the working rule of the lawyer. Its upper limit is
the philosopher's reasoned and rounded theory of
life. Between these extremes all the judgments that
men form about conduct fall within its scope.''[29]
''Blind adherence to custom is modified by an intelligent perception of the welfare of society, and moral
obligation is set upon a rational basis. These changes
react upon the actual contents of the moral law itself,
what is just and good in custom being sifted out
from what is indifferent or bad; and the purified
moral code reacts in turn on the legislation by which
advanced societies model their structure.''[30] It reacts
on legislation, but it reacts on judge-made law as
well. The moral code of each generation, this amal-
gam of custom and philosophy and many an intermediate grade of conduct and belief, supplies a
norm or standard of behavior which struggles to
make itself articulate in law. The sanction or source
of obligation for moral rules, it has been said,[31] is
the pressure of society on the individual mind.[32] The
same pressure is ever at work in the making of the
law declared by courts. The state in commissioning
its judges has commanded them to judge, but neither

[28] Hobhouse, *supra*, p. 18.
[29] Hobhouse, *supra*, p. 25.
[30] Hobhouse, *supra*, p. 30.
[31] Dewey, *Human Nature and Conduct*, pp. 326, 327; also pp.
75, 81.
[32] *Cf.* Korkunov, *General Theory of Law*, Modern Legal Phil.
Series, p. 45; Dewey and Tufts, *Ethics*, p. 360.

in constitution nor in statute has it formulated a
code to define the manner of their judging. The pressure of society invests new forms of conduct in the
minds of the multitude with the sanction of moral
obligation, and the same pressure working upon the
mind of the judge invests them finally through his
action with the sanction of the law.

Let me seek some illustrations of the movement of
judge-made law in accord with changing *mores*. The
law of domestic relations supplies the readiest examples. The husband at common law might restrain
his wife by force if there was danger of her leaving
him. There has been formal adjudication, if adjudication was needed to enlighten him, that the right is
gone today.[33] Gone is it with the yet more ancient
right, of which it was a phase, the right to maintain
the marital authority by moderate castigation. The
mores in their growth have imposed the restraint of
law upon these grosser acts of tyranny, and from
these has moved to others subtler and more elusive.
Cruelty was once identified with physical abuse. In-
sult and derision, mental torture as well as physical,
have come within its range.[34]

For society at large as well as for the family, the
changing *mores* have brought changing law. A new
sense of the significance of social solidarity has engendered a new conception of the duty to refrain
from anti-social conduct. Ancient precedents gave

[33] R. *v.* Jackson, 1891, 1 Q.B. 671.
[34] Pearson *v.* Pearson, 1920, 230 N.Y. 141.

support to the view that conduct harmful to one's neighbor did not depend for its legality upon the animating motive. Modern decisions have set bounds to the license theretofore accorded to "disinterested malevolence."[35] A growing altruism, or if not this, a growing sense of social interdependence, is at the bottom of the change. Power might be exercised with brutal indifference to the many when society was organized on a basis of special privilege for the few. Democracy has brought in its wake a new outlook, and with the new outlook a new law. The social forces contributing to the change did not write their message down into the set paragraphs of a statute. They left it in the air where the pressure was more effective because felt by all alike. At last, the message became law.

One gains the sense of an epic movement unifying the legal process, — the picture and the promise of a plot majestically unfolding itself amid all the interludes and diversions — when one reads the history of English law in its birthplace and across the seas. A study of Holdsworth's narrative in its monumental comprehensiveness has brought this sharply home to me. The latent energies within the legal system — what the ancients would have called its "entelechy" — are revealed in all their vigor. Some

[35] American Bank & Trust Co. *v.* Federal Reserve Bank, 1921, 256 U.S. 350, 358; Beardsley *v.* Kilmer, 1923, 236 N. Y. 80; Ames, *Lectures on Legal History*, p. 398; *cf.* however, Sorrell *v.* Smith, 1925, A.C. 700; Stammler, *The Theory of Justice*, Modern Legal Phil. Series, p. 253.

chapters have been told so often as to be familiar or
no longer strange. We have grown accustomed to the
significance of the forms of actions, and are no
longer surprised to hear that the doctrine of consideration might have been different if assumpsit
had not developed out of tort.[36] But there are other
principles, and weighty ones, where something other
than the forms of actions, more deliberate and conscious, has been the generative force. Take the rule
that a master is liable for the contracts and torts of
a servant within the scope of the apparent authority.
Could anything be more typical of the common law
as we know it? One has a shock of surprise when
one is told for the first time that as late as the seventeenth century the law was very different.[37] ''Except in those cases in which from motives of public
policy a more extended liability was allowed, a master was only liable for the acts of his agent if he had
actually ordered him to act, or if he had, by words or
conduct, subsequently ratified his acts.'' [38] There was
indeed a heavier liability for common carriers; for
householders whose servants had caused damage by
fire; and for the man who had undertaken to do
something, and by his servant had done it badly.[39]
But these and other instances of like liability were
departures from the general rule. Only about two
hundred years ago, at the end of the seventeenth

[36] Holdsworth, *History of English Law*, vol. 8, pp. 7, 42, 47.
[37] Holdsworth, *op. cit.*, vol. 8, pp. 227, 228, 229, 252, 474, 476.
[38] Holdsworth, *op. cit.*, vol. 8, p. 227.
[39] Holdsworth, *op. cit.*, vol. 8, p. 476; vol. 3, p. 385.

century, did judges awake to the fact that "the strict common law principles which governed the liability of masters or principals for the acts of their servants or agents were wholly unsuited to the commercial condition of the country."[40] They did not wait for legislation. Chief Justice Holt found in civil law principles, which had already been adopted by the Court of Admiralty, the analogies that were needed to smooth the path of progress. By borrowings from another system, with some infiltration of ideas from common law instances of exceptional liability, and if not thus, then at least by innovation of some sort, from whatever source derived, there came into English law the modern principle whereby the scope of the employer's liability is measured by the authority implicit in the nature of the business.[41] Only antiquarians recall that it is not as ancient as the law itself.

The powers inherent in the judicial office when Holt was Lord Chief Justice exist in undiminished force today. One does not extinguish them by saying that the earlier centuries were formative, and that there has followed a modern age in which the law is a closed book. Every age is modern to those who are living in it. True, of course, it is that in the centuries since Holt's time many lines once weak and wavering have become permanent and rigid. Principles and rules that were malleable in his day have petrified

40 Holdsworth, *op. cit.*, vol. 8, p. 252.
41 Holdsworth, *op. cit.*, vol. 8, pp. 229, 252, 474, 475; vol. 6, p. 520.

with the accumulated weight of precedent on precedent. Land within the territory of the law that was then unsettled or uncultivated has been peopled or reclaimed. Frontiers, however, there still are, and will always be, where the lines of demarcation are uncertain and debatable, where occupation, if any, has been provisional and timid, — borderlands and marches where minds impatient of injustice refuse to be held back, but point the pathway of advance into regions unexplored beyond. It may hearten spirits such as these to bear in mind the creative energies that dwelt within the legal system at the threshold of the modern era, two centuries ago.

The example supplied by Holt would have slight significance if it were singular. One can match it by many others. Take a case decided a century later, in 1789, the great case of Pasley *v.* Freeman.[42] The ruling was then made that an action in tort might be maintained for ''a false and fraudulent statement which caused damage to another, though there was no contractual relation between deceiver and the person deceived.''[43] One judge, Grose, J., dissented upon the ground that no precedent existed for ''an action upon a false affirmation, except against a party to a contract, and where there is a promise, either express or implied, that the fact is true which is misrepresented.'' Coming down to recent days, take the changes that have been wrought in the law

[42] 3 T.R. 51.
[43] Holdsworth, *op. cit.*, vol. 8, p. 426.

of defamation, of which two instances will suffice
among many that could be cited. Anciently the law
was that the mere repetition of a slander was not
actionable if the repetition was accompanied by a
designation of the author.[44] The common law world
was then a paradise for gossips. "This was long regarded as settled law [45] and was not overruled till
the beginning of the nineteenth century."[46] Within
the field of defamation, a second instance, yet more
recent, is furnished by the law of privilege. The fair
and true report of a judicial or other public proceed-
ing has long been held to be a privilege of the press.
At first, however, proceedings in courts not of record
were at times excluded from the privilege.[47] So were
ex parte proceedings. So were such proceedings as
the filing of a complaint or answer, at least until the
stage was reached when they laid a basis for judicial
actions. One by one these exceptions dropped away.
Proceedings in the lower courts were put on the same
footing as proceedings in the higher ones.[48] *Ex parte*
proceedings might be reported as freely as those
that were contentious.[49] Finally, only the other
day, the Court of Appeals of New York extended the
privilege to the report of statements in a pleading

[44] Earl of Northampton's Case, 1613, 2 Co. Rep. 134.
[45] Davis *v.* Lewis, 1796, 7 T.R. 17.
[46] McPherson *v.* Daniels, 1829, 10 B. & C. 263; Holdsworth, *op.
cit.*, vol. 8, p. 357.
[47] Odgers, *Libel and Slander*, 5th ed., p. 308.
[48] Odgers, *supra.*
[49] Usill *v.* Hales, 3 C.P.D. 324, 325; Wilson *v.* Walter, L.R., 4
Q.B. 93.

before the stage of trial.[50] "We may as well disregard the overwhelming weight of authority elsewhere," said Judge Pound, "and start with a rule of our own consistent with practical experience."[51] For example not less striking, take the group of decisions, the chief of them very recent, that revolutionized the law of blasphemy and the law of superstitious uses as they had stood in the English courts for three centuries and more.[52] "It is obvious," says Holdsworth, commenting on these decisions,[53] "that the dominant factor in the various trains of legal reasoning, which have justified the abolition of the older doctrines of law and equity, and, with the assistance of the Legislature, have impelled them in the direction of universal toleration, has been the influence of public opinion as to the proper relation of the state and its law to religion." There are observations in Lord Sumner's judgment in Bowman *v.* The Secular Society, *supra*, that may seem to disguise the transformation, or belittle its significance. "After all," he says,[54] "the question whether a given opinion is a danger to society is a question of the times, and is a question of fact." One may call it a question of fact if one will, for it is from the fact

[50] Campbell *v.* N. Y. Evening Post, 1927, 245 N.Y. 320.

[51] 245 N.Y. at p. 328; *cf.* remarks of Cockburn, C. J., in Wasson *v.* Walter, 1868, L.R., 4 Q.B. 73.

[52] R. *v.* Ramsay, 1883, 15 Cox, C. C. 231; Bowman *v.* The Secular Society, 1917, A.C. 406; Bowne *v.* Keane, 1919, A.C. 815; Holdsworth, *op. cit.*, vol. 8, pp. 415-420.

[53] P. 418.

[54] 1917, A.C. 466, 467.

that law emerges. "Ex facto jus oritur." [55] The truth is that a changing sense of the exactions of utility and justice has evoked a changing law.

Other illustrations are not lacking.[56] At times the new ethos does not mean that there has come into being a new conception of right and wrong. It may mean nothing more than a new impatience, a new restiveness, in the face of old abuses long recognized as wrong. Transition stages there are also when an observer can mark the law in the very process of "becoming." It is throwing off a crippling dogma, and struggling for freer motion. For years there has been a dogma of the books that in the absence of a special duty of protection, one may stand by with indifference and see another perish, by drowning, say, or fire, though there would be no peril in a rescue. A rule so divorced from morals was sure to breed misgivings. We need not be surprised to find that in cases of recent date, a tendency is manifest to narrow it or even whittle it away.[57] We cannot say today that the old rule has been supplanted. The rulings are too meagre. Sown, however, are the seeds of scepticism, the precursor often of decay. Some day

[55] *Cf.* Brandeis, J., in Adams *v.* Tanner, 1917, 244 U.S. 590, 600.

[56] One may find many of them in Lefroy, ''The Basis of Case Law,'' 22 *L.Q.R.* 293, and Andrews, ''Recent Decisions of the Court of Appeals,'' 12 *Cornell Law Quarterly* 433.

[57] Pound, *Law and Morals*, pp. 72, 73; and *cf.* his citation of Bentham, *Principles of Morals and Legislation*, ch. 17, sec. 19, Clarendon Press Edition, p. 323; Lefroy, ''The Basis of Case Law,'' 22 *L.Q.R.* 293; Queen *v.* Instan, 1893, 1 Q.B. 450.

we may awake to find that the old tissues are dissolved. Then will come a new generalization, and with it a new law.[58]

Our course of advance, therefore is neither a straight line nor a curve. It is a series of dots and

[58] A significant case is Queen *v.* Instan, 1893, 1 Q.B. 450. There, the defendant, a woman of full age and having no means of her own, lived alone with her aunt, a woman of seventy-three, who maintained her. The aunt for the last ten days of her life suffered from a disease which made her perfectly helpless. During this time the defendant lived in the house, and took in the food supplied by the tradesmen, but gave none of it to the sick woman, and procured neither nursing nor medical attendance. Death was accelerated by lack of food and care. The Queen's Bench Division unanimously decided that a duty was imposed on the defendant under the circumstances to supply her aunt with sufficient food to maintain life, and she was convicted of manslaughter. Lord Coleridge, C.J., said (p. 453): "It would not be correct to say that every moral obligation involves a legal duty; but every legal duty is founded on a moral obligation. A legal common law duty is nothing else than the enforcing by law of that which is a moral obligation without legal enforcement. There can be no question in this case that it was the clear duty of the prisoner to impart to the deceased so much as was necessary to sustain life of the food which she from time to time took in and which was paid for by the deceased's own money for the purpose of maintenance of herself and the prisoner; it was only through the instrumentality of the prisoner that the deceased could get the food. There was therefore a common law duty imposed upon the prisoner which she did not discharge. . . . There is no case directly in point; but it would be a slur upon and a discredit to the administration of justice in this country if there were any doubt as to the legal principle, or as to the present case being within it. The prisoner was under a moral obligation to the deceased from which arose a legal duty towards her."

Casuistry will discover reasons why the holding in that case falls short of a decision that a stranger to one in danger may be charged with a legal duty of succor or of rescue. The holding is none the less significant of a tendency of thought which is gaining year by year in power and momentum.

dashes. Progress comes *per saltum*, by successive
compromises between extremes, compromises often,
if I may borrow Professor Cohen's phrase, between
"positivism and idealism." "The notion that a
jurist can dispense with any consideration as to
what the law ought to be arises from the fiction that
the law is a complete and closed system, and that
judges and jurists are mere automata to record its
will or phonographs to pronounce its provisions." [59]
Ideas of justice will no more submit to be "banished
from the theory of law" than "from its administration." [60] "What has happened," we are told, "is
simply that ideas of justice have lost prestige among
jurists and are pursued in an unavowed form." [61]

I take leave to doubt whether the prestige of idealism as one of the motive forces of the law is indeed
at so low an ebb. If I were to state the case in terms
of the tides, I would say that a flood season is at
hand, if not already here.[62] Juristic idealism, as I
view the scene, is more conscious of itself than it has
been for many years. Jurists such as Stammler in
Germany and Geny in France have brought it forth
into the open when once it was concealed. Whatever
its prestige, and however unavowed its processes,
there can be little doubt as to its power. You may

[59] Morris R. Cohen, "Positivism and the Limits of Idealism in
the Law," 27 *Columbia Law Review* 237, 238.

[60] *Ibid.*

[61] *Ibid.*, p. 237.

[62] *Cf.* Cardozo, "A Ministry of Justice," 35 *Harv. L. Rev.* 113, at
p. 126.

chain the law down with all manner of clamps and bonds. The wizard Justice has a queer way of setting the victim free. This is true even in systems founded upon codes. It is more plainly true of a system such as ours. Even in code systems, the law leaves many things unsaid. It states a general principle, and turns over to the judge the task of filling up the gaps.[63] His guide is then the just law, the law, that is to say, whereby justice is attained. The positive law may indeed override the law of justice. "We must always remember," says Stammler, "that the judge has a right to introduce and exercise just law directly, only in those cases where the positive law directs him to do so."[64] The direction may be implied, however, as well as express. "The positive law may lay this duty upon him by explicit instruction or by silence."[65] In case of the law's silence, we must have recourse to the fundamental idea of law itself, "an endeavor to realize justice by force."[66] Often, however, the reference to the just law is explicit and unmistakable. Take, for instance, the provisions of Sec. 242 of the German Civil Code:[67] "The debtor is obliged to perform his service as good faith and

[63] Stammler, *Theory of Justice*, Modern Legal Phil. Series, 198, 199; Vinogradoff, *Historical Jurisprudence*, vol. 2, pp. 64, 65, citing Aristotle's *Rhetoric*.

[64] P. 240; *cf.* Brütt, *Die Kunst der Rechtsanwendung*, p. 147.

[65] P. 241.

[66] P. 209; *cf.* Brütt, *op. cit.*, p. 163: "Sehr zahlreich sind die Fälle, in denen unser Recht unmittelbar auf richtiges Recht Bezug nimmt."

[67] *Bürgerliches Gesetzbuch.*

regard to business custom dictate." There is a like
provision in the French Code Civil.[68] We must not
think of the just law, when it prevails, as something
distinct from the positive law, or in antagonism to it.
It is itself a phase, a subdivision, a compartment, of
positive law. As to this Stammler is at pains to develop his thesis with precision. There is a very general "misapprehension," he says,[69] "of the concepts
positive and just law." "It seems" to many "that
there is a distinction between positive law and a certain 'ethical something' which, at any rate, is not
law. This is not true. The distinction we are making
is within law itself. It refers to the difference in the
manner in which the 'content' of 'positive' law is to
be determined. They are merely different means with
which the one positive law intends to carry out its
fundamental purpose. Accordingly 'good faith' is
not outside of positive law; much less is it opposed
to it; but it is an instrument of the positive law which
the latter employs to determine its content."

If a code does not escape the need of supplement-
ing its mandates by reference to the norms of morals,
we may be sure that the same instrument of growth
in the hands of common law judges will be used with
greater freedom. The whole system which they develop has been built on the assumption that it is an
expression of the *mores*. What has once been settled
by a precedent will not be unsettled over night, for

[68] Sections 1134, 1359.
[69] P. 259.

certainty and uniformity are gains not lightly to be sacrificed. Above all is this true when honest men have shaped their conduct upon the faith of the pronouncement. On the other hand, conformity is not to be turned into a fetich. The disparity between precedent and ethos may so lengthen with the years that only covin and chicanery would be disappointed if the separation were to end. There are many intermediate stages, moreover, between adherence and reversal. The pressure of the *mores,* if inadequate to obliterate the past, may fix direction for the future. The evil precedent may live, but so sterilized and truncated as to have small capacity for harm. It will be prudently ignored when invoked as an apposite analogy in novel situations, though the novel element be small. There will be brought forward other analogies, less precise, it may be, but more apposite to the needs of morals. The weights are constantly shifted to restore the equilibrium between precedent and justice.

II

The Meaning of Justice — The Science of Values

If justice has this place in shaping the pathway of the law, it will profit us to know what justice means. ''What we are seeking is not merely the justice that one receives when his rights and duties are determined by the law as it is; what we are seeking is the justice to which law in its making should conform.''[70] Stammler in his *Theory of Justice* draws a sharp distinction between the law of justice and morality. His view is the Kantian one that morality is concerned with the purity of the will.[71] The just law, on the contrary, has relation to acts. From this it follows, he argues [72] that ''no matter how far the ethical perfection of the human race may in the course of time advance, there will always remain the right rule of social life as a specific object of investigation. The technical possibilities, the changing qualities and capabilities, the external conditions of life in the different regions of the world, — all of these offer a peculiar basis for coöperation, which must be regulated. And this regulation forms the object of an

[70] Cardozo, *Growth of the Law*, p. 87.
[71] Stammler, *op. cit.*, pp. 40, 54, 58.
[72] P. 55.

31

independent method and study. A merely technical economy cannot be managed directly by the principles of good intention and perfection of character if we are to obtain final results. Our problems are of such a nature that we must first master them by means of rules for external conduct.'' There are, of course, other students of ethics who reject the Kantian principle that acts have no ethical quality in and of themselves apart from the will of the actor. ''Most people,'' says Spencer,[73] ''regard the subject matter of Ethics as being conduct considered as calling forth approbation or reprobation. But the primary subject matter of Ethics is conduct considered objectively as producing good or bad results to self or others or both.'' This was Bentham's thesis: ''If motives are good or bad, it is only on account of their effects.''[74] So today in the school of thinkers known as the English neo-realists, of whom George E. Moore is a notable example, goodness is held to be an ultimate and objectively subsisting entity.[75] In this view, the just law as Stammler conceives it becomes identified with the moral law, or with so much of the moral law as defines the quality of justice.

I must leave it to students of ethics to choose between these conflicting schools of thought, or to trace, as some have tried to do, a reconciling path of

[73] *Principles of Ethics*, part ii, ''Justice,'' sec. 246.
[74] *Principles of Morals and Legislation*, ch. x, sec. 2.
[75] Moore, *Ethics*, Home University Library; A. K. Rogers, *English and American Philosophy Since 1800*, p. 143.

compromise that will utilize what is true in each, and avoid their common error.[76] The student of legal science will fall back upon a method familiar to the law, and not unknown to philosophy. A German philosopher, Hans Vaihinger, has written a book which he has called *The Philosophy of As If, Die Philosophie des Als Ob.* "I called this work," he says,[77] "*The Philosophy of As If* because it seemed to me to express more convincingly than any other possible title what I wanted to say, namely that 'As If,' *i.e.*, appearance, the consciously false, plays an enormous part in science, in world philosophies and in life. I wanted to give a complete enumeration of all the methods in which we operate intentionally with consciously false ideas, or rather judgments. I wanted to reveal the secret life of these extraordinary methods. I wanted to give a complete theory, an anatomy and physiology, so to speak, or rather a biology of 'As If.' " Adam Smith, for illustration, was a disciple of the philosophy of "As If" when he built a science of political economy on the assumption of an economic man, animated by egoism to the exclusion of all other impulses, and by that particular aspect of egoism which aims at economic good. There is no occasion, however, for going afield, and gathering illustrations from sciences other than our own. The law is no stranger to the philosophy of "As If." It has built up many of its doctrines by a make-

76 Dewey and Tufts, *Ethics*, pp. 237, 238.
77 Ogden's Translations, *The Philosophy of As If*, p. xli.

believe that things are other than they are. I put aside for the moment the crasser forms of fiction that have played a part upon the legal scene; for example, an allegation in a pleading not subject to be traversed, and yet known to be untrue. For the most part they were devices to advance the ends of justice, yet clumsy and at times offensive. Indeed, the father of Sir Matthew Hale gave up the practice of the law "because he could not reconcile his conscience to the system of adding untrue allegations to pleadings so as to 'lend colour' to the proceedings." [78] These forms are out of date, but we have with us even now, the quasi-contract, the adopted child, the constructive trust, all of flourishing vitality, to attest the empire of "as if" today. What I have in mind more particularly, however, is a class of fictions of another order, the fiction which is a working tool of thought, but which at times hides itself from view till reflection and analysis have brought it to the light. As political economy has its economic man, so jurisprudence has its reasonable man, its negligent man, and, what is more in point for us just now, its moral man. Professor Edgerton in a recent paper has reviewed the authorities that bear upon the distinction between subjective and objective negligence. With a wealth of illustration he has developed the thesis that "negligence neither is nor involves ('presupposes') either indifference or inadvertence, or any other mental characteristic, qual-

[78] Birkenhead, *Fourteen English Judges*, p. 53.

ity, state or process. Negligence is unreasonably dangerous conduct — *i.e.*, conduct abnormally likely to cause harm. Freedom from negligence (commonly called 'due care') does not require care, or any other mental phenomenon, but requires only that one's conduct be reasonably safe — as little likely to cause harm as the conduct of a normal person would be.'' [79] The law maintains this objective outlook upon morals to the extent that it appropriates the norms of morals as its own. The pure will may serve as an *excuse* when will or intention is the essence of a wrong.[80] It is not equivalent without more to the attainment of the moral ideal so far as that ideal is also the criterion of law. The jural pattern of moral values is the conduct that is moral in any given situation when the actor is viewed ''als ob,'' as if, endowed with normal powers of will and understanding. The law may be satisfied with less. It does not aspire to less. It looks to nothing lower, but also perhaps to nothing higher, in framing its ideal.

I come back then to the definition of justice considered as a jural norm. It may be narrower or broader than the specific quality of justice as known to ethical theory. I hold it for my part to be so much of morality as juristic thought discovers to be wisely and efficiently enforcible by the aid of jural sanctions. I have little help here from Stammler's ex-

[79] Edgerton, ''Negligence, Inadvertence and Indifference,'' 39 *Harv. L. R.* 849.

[80] See *e.g.*, ''Director of Public Prosecutions *v.* Beard,'' 1920, A.C. 479; Holdsworth, *op. cit.*, vol. 8, p. 443.

position and analysis. Summary of his theory would be profitless, for the meaning is unintelligible without ample illustration.[81] His definition when developed is not lacking in suggestive power. It is too vague, however, and too abstract, to be a crutch for limping minds.[82] I think the law does better when it adopts another method of approach more pragmatic and inductive. One who seeks examples of this method will find them in the writings of Lévy-Bruhl among the French and in those of Hobhouse among the English.[83] "The morals of any given society at any given epoch," says Lévy-Bruhl,[84] "are determined by the totality of its conditions both from a static and a dynamic view point." "Social justice is a 'becoming,' if not a continuous progress." [85] "The content of the moral ideal is thus a compound of imagination, tradition and observation of social realities." [86] We have already followed the same thought in Hobhouse. The standards are the product of an interaction between impulse and habit,[87] and again between custom and reflection.

It comes down to this. There are certain forms of

[81] One will find a useful summary of Stammler's thought in Hocking, *Law and Rights.*

[82] *Cf.* Kaufmann, "Der Kritik der Neukantischen Rechtsphilosophie," pp. 11, 16, *Tübingen,* 1921.

[83] Lévy-Bruhl, *La Morale et la Science des Moeurs*; Hobhouse, *Morals in Evolution*; *cf.*, Demogue, *op. cit.,* 7 Modern Legal Phil. Series, pp. 376, 378.

[84] *Op. cit.,* p. 197.

[85] P. 213.

[86] P. 151.

[87] Dewey, *Human Nature and Conduct.*

conduct which at any given place and epoch are commonly accepted under the combined influence of reason, practice and tradition, as moral or immoral. If we were asked to define the precise quality that leads them to be so characterized, we might find it troublesome to make answer, yet the same difficulty is found in defining other abstract qualities, even those the most familiar. The forms of conduct thus discriminated are not the same at all times or in all places. Law accepts as the pattern of its justice the morality of the community whose conduct it assumes to regulate. In saying this, we are not to blind ourselves to the truth that uncertainty is far from banished. Morality is not merely different in different communities. Its level is not the same for all the component groups within the same community. A choice must still be made between one group standard and another. We have still to face the problem, at which one of these levels does the social pressure become strong enough to convert the moral norm into a jural one? All that we can say is that the line will be higher than the lowest level of moral principle and practice, and lower than the highest. The law will not hold the crowd to the morality of saints and seers. It will follow, or strive to follow, the principle and practice of the men and women of the community whom the social mind would rank as intelligent and virtuous.

The question then is whether the justice to which the law aspires is to be identified with virtue generally or only with some phase of it. Many attempts

have been made to isolate the quality of justice, and,
stripped of other forms of virtue, to make it the ideal
of law.[88] Plato saw in justice the harmony of the soul,
which made it one with virtue generally.[89] Aristotle
identified virtue with the mean between extremes,
and saw in justice only a phase of it, the quality of
virtue whereby every man receives his due. The difficulty is only cloaked, for what is due must be defined.[90] Yet Aristotle did not stop with the notion of
mere legality. The jural ideal was felt even then to
be justice thus limited and also something more.
What is most significant in Aristotle's treatment of
the subject is his chapter on a kind of justice which
he describes as a justice outside legality,[91] δικαιοσύνη
is to be supplemented by ἐπιείκεια, law by equity, the
rule by the humane exception. ''The teaching on this
department of justice forms one of the most instructive parts of Greek jurisprudence; it has had a long
history and a great influence on modern develop-
ments of the theory of law.'' [92] We get the same
thought in the chapters of the *Ethics* that deal with
other virtues. ''That principle,'' says Aristotle,
''which is most truly just is thought to partake of the

[88] Cardozo, *The Growth of the Law*, p. 86.

[89] Hobhouse, *Morals in Evolution*, p. 554; Archibald Alexander, *A Short History of Philosophy*, p. 57; Plato, *The Republic*, Book iv, sec. 443 (p. 149, Golden Treasury ed.).

[90] *Cf.* Cohen, ''Positivism and the Limits of Idealism in the Law,'' 27 *Col.L.R.* 237, 240.

[91] Vinogradoff, *Historical Jurisprudence*, vol. ii, p. 63; Aristotle, *Nicomachean Ethics*, Everyman's ed.. pp. 126, 127.

[92] Vinogradoff, *op. cit.*, p. 63.

nature of friendship.''[93] The stranger within the gates becomes a neighbor or a friend.

Among the moderns, Spencer announced a formula of justice, ''Every man is free to do that which he wills, provided he infringes not the equal freedom of any other man.'' [94] This is in effect to make justice one with liberty. Stammler in his analysis of Justice [95] introduces the conception of grace or leniency as Aristotle had done before him, but ends with the Kantian ideal of a freely developed and freely acting personality. So, in our own body of law, the standard to which we appeal is sometimes characterized as that of justice, but also as the equitable, the fair, the thing consistent with good conscience.[96]

An ideal so expansive is no longer capable of being compressed within the analogy of an account between a debtor and a creditor with justice as the *quid pro quo*. The jural as well as the moral norm of justice, or even more perhaps than the moral norm, has in it an infusion of qualities with which justice is at times contrasted, such as charity or compas-

[93] *Nicomachean Ethics*, Bk. viii, Everyman's ed., p. 183; *cf.* p. 197.

[94] *Principles of Ethics*, part ii, ''Justice,'' sec. 272; *cf.* Small, *General Sociology*, p. 603. For other definitions, see Demogue, *Analysis of Fundamental Notions*, vol. 7, Modern Legal Philosophy Series, pp. 481, 482, 483, 493, 494; Cardozo, *The Growth of the Law*, pp. 86, 87.

[95] *Op. cit.*, pp. 94, 193.

[96] Haines, ''The Law of Nature in Federal Decisions,'' 25 *Yale Law Journal* 617. For a recent illustration, see Yome *v.* Gorman, 1926, 242 N.Y. 396, 402, 404.

sion.[97] One who makes a payment carelessly has himself to blame for his plight if the payment is too large. Even so, the bank paying by mistake a check drawn by its customer in excess of the balance in his account, may at times get the money back from a payee, a third party, who acted in good faith.[98] Ownership is divested out of pity for negligence or error. One who sells his inheritance improvidently under the pressure of immediate need, knows that by the terms of the sale he gives up the expectancy forever. Even so, the buyer may be compelled (at least in many jurisdictions) to exhibit an involuntary charity and refrain from taking advantage of the necessities of the seller.[99] One who is in lawful possession of land may expel the unwelcome visitor, who, when bidden to depart, remains, and still more the intruder who has entered without leave. Even so, the privilege may vanish if the visitor is ill so that expulsion would be dangerous, or if the intruder has moored his boat at the dock to seek shelter in a storm.[100] One who holds over in possession of a building after the expiration of a term of years may be deemed at the election of the landlord to be a tenant for another

[97] *Cf.* Dewey and Tufts, *Ethics*, p. 415.

[98] F. N. Bk. *v.* Carnegie Trust Co., 1915, 213 N.Y. 301, 306; Mt. Morris Bank *v.* 23rd Ward Bank, 1902, 172 N.Y. 244.

[99] Pomeroy, *Equity Jurisprudence*, sec. 953.

[100] Depue *v.* Flatau, 100 Minn. 299; Ploff *v.* Putnam, 81 Vt. 471; Vincent *v.* Lake Erie Transp. Co., 109 Minn. 456; Bohlen, ''Incomplete Privilege to Commit Intention Invasions of Property and Personality,'' 39 *Harvard L.R.* 301.

year.[101] Even so, the holding-over may be unavailing
to lay a basis for the election when the tenant has
been ill so that it would have been dangerous to
leave.[102] Shylock appealed to justice, yet Portia
made us know that the jural norm, however much it
might disguise itself under a strict construction of
the bond, did not in truth ignore the quality of
mercy.[103] If this is true at times when the remedies
are legal and enforcible of right, it is true even of-
tener when the remedies are equitable and enforcible
at discretion. At the basis of the law of contract is
the maxim *"uti lingua nuncupassit, ita jus esto."*[104]
This is the foundation, yet many pages have been
written to show the remedies available when the
tongue has made a slip. There are other situations in
which there figures even more plainly the element of
grace. A contract is made without fraud or oppression. Change of circumstances brings hardship. The
Chancellor withholds his remedies, and remits the
suitor to a claim for damages which is known to be
futile. Justice again is done by making charity a
duty.

There must be flexibility for the formula that will
hold within its walls this thing of changing content.
Justice as a jural norm is not a fixed or determinate
phase of the totality of moral conduct in a given situation. On the other hand, it is not morality as a

101 Schuyler *v.* Smith, 1873, 51 N.Y. 309.
102 Herter *v.* Mullen, 1899, 159 N.Y. 28.
103 *Cf.* Jhering, *The Struggle for Law*, Lalor's translation, p. 81.
104 Stammler, *op. cit.*, p. 300.

whole, even objectively considered. It is so much of
morality as the thought and practice of a given
epoch shall conceive to be appropriately invested
with a legal sanction, and thereby marked off from
morality in general.[105] This is not unlike the doctrine
taught by Jellinek, though there are elements of difference. "Law" in his teaching "is a minimum
ethics, that is to say the whole combined require-
ments of morals, whose observance, at a given stage
of social development is absolutely indispensable."[106]
If for "law" we substitute some such term as "the
jural norm of justice," we shall not be far away from
truth. I do not mean that judges have it in their
power at one sweep to bring the law as it exists into
conformity with this provisional ideal. Advance even
so far may mean innovation too radical to be effected
in a day without the aid of legislation. I mean that
the ideal is nothing less, though the law of any epoch
will always be behind it. If I may borrow a metaphor
from the law of waters, the process by which judges
work is one of erosion rather than avulsion. Here a
little and there a little. We look about us later, and
behold, the waste places are reclaimed.[107] Legal custom develops by the same forces and methods that

[105] *Cf.*, Pound, *Law and Morals*, p. 111; Duguit, *Traité de Droit
Constitutionnel*, vol. i, pp. 36, 41; Cardozo, *Growth of the Law*, p. 49.

[106] Korkunov, *General Theory of Law*, p. 61; Pound, *Law and
Morals*, p. 110.

[107] The thought is happily expressed by Street, *Foundation of
Legal Liability*, vol. i, p. 499: "Development there must be. But it
cannot take place by leaps and bounds. There must be no ellipsis of
any intermediate process. In the course of legal growth older princi-

build up custom generally. "We know," says Hobhouse in his *Morals in Evolution*,[108] "how customs change and grow and disappear unconsciously as an individual stretches a point here or makes a new application of a precedent there. We can see how the interaction of multitudinous forces transmutes custom and produces a new tradition before any one has been aware of the change." So with the growth of law. The judge stretches a point here in response to a moral urge, or makes a new application of a precedent there. Before long a new tradition has arisen. Duties that had been conceived of as moral only, without other human sanction than the opinion of society, are found to be such that they may effectively and wisely be subjected to another form of sanction, the power of society. The moral norm and the jural have been brought together, and are one.

With some elements of difference, this conception of justice as legally organized or organizable morality is akin to the idea of justice as it has been analyzed by Mill. "Now it is known," he says in his essay "Utilitarianism,"[109] "that ethical writers divide moral duties into two classes, denoted by the ill-chosen expressions, duties of perfect and of imperfect obligation; the latter being those in which, though the act is obligatory, the particular occasions of performing it are left to our choice; as in the case

ples are transcended, but this must take place by steps so natural and inevitable as to be in a measure unconscious."

[108] P. 616.

[109] Everyman's edition, p. 46.

of charity or beneficence, which we are indeed bound to practice, but not towards any definite person, nor at any prescribed time. In the more precise language of philosophic jurists, duties of perfect obligation are those duties in virtue of which a correlative *right* resides in some person or persons; duties of imperfect obligation are those moral obligations which do not give rise to any right. I think it will be found that this distinction exactly coincides with that which exists between justice and the other obligations of morality. In our survey of the various popular acceptations of justice, the term appeared generally to involve the idea of a personal right — a claim on the part of one or more individuals, like that which the law gives when it confers a proprietary or other legal right. Whether the injustice consists in depriving a person of a possession, or in breaking faith with him, or in treating him worse than he deserves, or worse than other people who have no greater claims, in each case the supposition implies two things — a wrong done and some assignable person who is wronged. Injustice may also be done by treating a person better than others; but the wrong in this case is to his competitors, who are also assignable persons. It seems to me that this feature in the case — a right in some person correlative to the moral obligation — constitutes the specific difference between justice and generosity or beneficence. Justice implies something which it is not only right to do, and wrong not to do, but which some individual

person can claim from us as his moral right.'' Mill
goes on to point out that ''no one has a moral right
to our generosity or beneficence, because we are not
morally bound to practice those virtues toward any
given individual.'' There are times, however, as I
have sought to show, when we are so bound — when
the virtue of benevolence loses its indeterminate
quality, and connotes the existence of a correlative
claim of right. To that extent it is annexed to the
domain of justice, and is incorporated into the jural
norm.

Whenever a relation between human beings becomes organized into one that is specifically jural,
the duties attached to it by law are assimilated more
and more to those attached to it by morals. The law
will not command the rich to give alms to the indi-
gent. On occasion, none the less, it will impose restraints upon power taking advantage of necessity.
The law will not enforce a duty of kindness to a
neighbor. It will enforce a duty of kindness to wife
or child or pupil. Observe, however, that relations,
once so vague and unorganized as to lack a jural
quality, may become organized and definite with the
result that thereafter rights and duties will belong
to them. A new relation may be established, or at
times an existing one extended. For many years,
there was stress upon a relation known as privity.
In default of that connecting bond, there were times
when the law would not recognize duties that were
recognized in morals. Decisions of recent date have

made the bond of diminishing importance, and have broadened the relations to one's fellows from which duties are engendered.[110] The scope of legal duty has expanded in obedience to the urge of morals. We see the same urge in decisions that charge an owner of land with special duties to the young and heedless.[111] We see it in the inroad made by recent cases upon the concept of an infant's disability where injustice would be wrought if the concept were maintained in all its rigorous simplicity.[112] We see it in a tendency, still almost in embryo, and yet perceptible, to enlarge the duties owing to licensees and even trespassers by a gradual extension of the class of invitees.[113] We see it in the striking growth of the concept of duress, a concept broad enough today to supply a remedy against unfairness and oppression in forms long ranked as guiltless.[114] At times, indeed, the movement has been helped by legislation. The land owner was without redress at common law if

[110] Cardozo, *The Growth of the Law*, p. 77; *cf.* Int. Prod. Co. *v.* Erie R. R. Co., 1927, 244 N.Y. 331.

[111] R. R. Co. *v.* Stout, 17 Wall. 657; U. P. R. Co. *v.* McDonald, 152 U.S. 262; Glasgow Corp. *v.* Taylor, 1922, A C. 1; Perry *v.* Rochester Line Co., 1916, 219 N.Y. 60, 65; *contra*, Walsh *v.* Fitchburgh R. R. Co., 1895, 145 N.Y. 301; and *cf.* United Zinc & Capital Co. *v.* Britt, 1922, 258 U.S. 268.

[112] Rice *v.* Butler, 1899, 160 N.Y. 578; Myers *v.* Hurley Motor Co., 1927, 273 U.S. 18; *contra*, McCarthy *v.* Henderson, 138 Mass. 310.

[113] Pompana *v.* N. Y. Ry. Co., 66 Conn. 538, 539; Glasgow Corp. *v.* Taylor, 1922 A.C. 1; Shearman and Redfield, *Negligence*, 6th ed., sec. 706.

[114] See, *e.g.*, Buckley *v.* Mayor, 30 App. Div. 463; 1899, 159 N. Y. 558.

his neighbor cut off his light and air for the mere purpose of annoyance.[115] Statutes against spite fences have made neighborliness a duty.[116] Yet there are fields not far removed where statutes have been needless. In economic rivalry, the trader or the merchant may be ungenerous toward his competitor to promote his own advancement. He goes too far if the animating motive is unadulterated malice, the mere desire to destroy.[117]

Such are present-day distinctions. We must be on our guard against supposing that they have the attribute of finality. Stammler in his discussion of the German Civil Code [118] insists that the rule of justice should do more than forbid the unneighborly act that is animated by malice. In his view there should be a positive duty of generous conduct, when there would be no loss to the doer or loss proportionately trivial. Undoubtedly the moral norm is not satisfied with less. The time may come when the jural norm will be able to exact as much. For the transformation that comes from the steady pressure of the *mores* is like the fabled transformation of the poet's dream. He awoke and found it truth. The standards of legal justice have been moved while we were dreaming of them, and planted in new soil. I speak of the standards as those of justice, yet it is justice in a large

115 Phelps *v.* Nowlen, 1878, 72 N.Y. 39.

116 Rideout *v.* Knox, 148 Mass. 368.

117 *Ante*, p. 14; *cf.* Exchange Bakery *v.* Rifpin, 1927, 245 N.Y. 260, 263.

118 *Op. cit.*, p. 253.

sense, δικαιοσύνη modified by ἐπιείκεια, by the softer
virtue of grace or leniency. The jural norm is identified with so much of the moral norm as exerts upon
the social mind a pressure too strong to be satisfied
with the sanction of mere opinion. A response or re-
action is evoked in the form of social sentiment and
conviction from which emerges a demand that the
sanction of the opinion of society shall be fortified
by the sanction of its power. When this pressure has
gone so far that it may no longer be resisted, the
judges are to say. For that they are interpreters of
the social mind, its will, its expectation, its desires.''[119] They tell us when the norms and standards of behavior and opinion have become so organized through the forces of custom or of morals as to
have become translated into law. ''Claims,'' says
Vinogradoff in his lectures on Custom and Right,[120]
''are made every day in all possible directions, and
out of claims there arise sometimes what may be
called natural claims, or moral rights. A man who
has conferred a benefit on another person, even if he
has no kind of written and valid acknowledgment in
regard to the obligee, may rightly say that he has a
claim to the gratitude or to reciprocal services of the
other party. In order that such a moral claim should
become juridical, it must pass through a second
stage, the stage of declaration of right. A declaration of right is the admission by organized society

[119] Lefroy, ''The Basis of Case Law,'' 22 *Law Quart. Rev.* 293,
302, 303.
[120] P. 68.

that the claim is justified from the public point of view.'' [121] Organized society may speak in such matters by the voice of its representatives in legislative assemblies. It may speak, at least in our Anglo-American system, by the voice of its judges. ''The gradual consolidation of opinions and habits'' [122] will then have done its work, and to the sanction of their pressure will be added the sanction of the law.

I have spoken of judges as the interpreters of the ''social mind.'' There are possibilities of much logomachy in such a form of words. I have no desire to invite them. Among students of social theory there are some who view the mind of society as something super-added to the minds of the component members.[123] Other students tell us that the social mind, if we are to use the term at all, is merely the sum of individual minds acting in society.[124] My own point of view will become clearer perhaps when I shall have occasion to discuss the antithesis between the individual and the group. I put aside for the moment the endless conflict between the monists and the pluralists, between the nominalists and the real-

---

[121] *Cf.* Duguit, *Traité de Droit Constitutionnel*, vol. 1, p. 361.

[122] Vinogradoff, *op. cit.*, p. 21.

[123] Cooley, *Social Organization*; Maitland, Introduction to Gierke's *Political Theory of the Middle Age*, xviii; *cf.* Hocking, *Man and the State*, p. 351; Borchard, ''Government Responsibility in Tort,'' 36 *Yale L.J.* 757, 774.

[124] Perry, *General Theory of Value*, pp. 461, 462, 465, 467; Mac-Iver, *The Modern State*, pp. 449, 452, 474; Laski, *Grammar of Politics*, p. 32; Hobhouse, *Social Evolution and Political Theory*, p. 87; Giddings, *The Principles of Sociology*, p. 132.

ists, obtruding itself here as upon so many scenes of
carnage. We can be indifferent for present purposes
whether the social mind is to be reckoned as unitary
or multiple. Let it stand for nothing more than the
organ or organs, whether they be multiple or unitary, out of which public opinion emerges as a product. Mr. Lippmann has taught us that the product
is often put before us with spurious marks and sym-
bols, so that recognition of its quality is at times no
easy task.[125] Still more recently Dr. Dewey in his
lectures, ''The Public and its Problems,'' has been
preaching the same lesson. Indeed, there is an am-
biguity in the very word ''public,'' for the thought to
be appraised and heeded is not the hasty or uncon-
sidered impressions of the crowd; it is the thought
of those sections of the crowd whose impressions
have ripened into genuine opinion.[126] ''The public is
not, as I see it,'' says Mr. Lippmann, ''a fixed body
of individuals.'' [127] So it is that Giddings bids us to
distinguish sharply ''between public opinion and
popular opinions and beliefs, and defines public
opinion as critically thought out social judgments.'' [128] Opinion is not the commonplace, — at

[125] Lippmann, ''Public Opinion,'' ''Liberty and the News,'' ''The
Phantom Public,'' *passim.*

[126] *Cf.* Cardozo, *The Nature of the Judicial Process,* pp. 108-111.

[127] Lippmann, *The Phantom Public,* p. 77; *cf.* pp. 168, 198; Hobhouse, *supra*; also Dewey, *The Public and its Problems,* pp. 116, 117,
123, 126, 177; and Lowell, *Public Opinion and Popular Government,*
pp. 13, 15; C. H. Cooley, *Social Organizations,* p. 121.

[128] Giddings, *Inductive Sociology,* quoted by Barnes, *Sociology and
Political Theory,* p. 202.

least not by any law inherent in its being. "One mind
in the right, whether in statesmanship, science,
morals, or what not, may raise all other minds to its
own point of view." [129] We do not strike an average
between the thoughts of ability and folly.[130] If it is
not the commonplace, still less is it the hasty prepossession, the whim or humor of the hour. Rather are
we to identify it with that "strong and preponderant
opinion" which has capacity at times to turn desire
into law.[131] The common will must have made itself
known for so long a time as well as in so distinct a
manner as to have gained stability and authority.[132]

I do not underrate the blindness of the manuscript,
the need of circumspection in deciphering its char-
acters, the manifold possibilities of error when every precept of caution has been formulated and followed. The task, however difficult, is here, and one
must discharge it as one can. Legislators, confronted
with a problem that differs in degree rather than in
kind, solve or attempt to solve it day by day, with
varying success, but at least with no thought to give
it up at the beginning. Read such a book as the *Rise
of American Civilization*, by Charles and Mary
Beard, and see how the surge of social forces has

129 Cooley, *op. cit.*, p. 124; Hobhouse, *supra.*

130 "Quid turpius quam sapientis vitam ex insipientium sermone
pendere?" Cicero, *De Finibus*, Book II, xv (Loeb's *Classical Library*,
p. 138).

131 Holmes, J., in Noble State Bank *v.* Haskell, 219 U.S. 104.

132 *Cf.*, W. H. Taft, *Popular Government*, quoted by Dickinson,
*Administrative Justice and the Supremacy of Law in the United
States*, p. 103; also Lowell, *op. cit.*, pp. 13, 15, 24, 46.

swept aside the little eddies of faction, the currents of party politics, or caught them in its larger movement.[133] Measures the most distinctive and important have taken form in obedience to a pressure that has overwhelmed the lines of sect or party; they are the emanation of a will which has become composite and impersonal. Not less clamorous at times is the summons to the courts to scan the scroll of life and announce their readings to the world.

In my discussion of the legal norms and of their gradual discovery and erection through the methods of the judicial process, I have isolated the quality of justice, and viewed it as if the search to understand and declare it were something singular and special. In truth the search is but a phase of a wider effort, a stage of a longer movement, a fragment of a larger whole. We read the quality of legal justice in the disclosures of the social mind. We read in the same book the values of all the social interests, moral, economic, educational, scientific, or aesthetic. A new science, the science of values or axiology·is teaching students of social problems to read the book aright. A copious literature is already at their service. Such books as Bouglé's *Evolution of Values* (well translated by Mrs. Sellars), Perry's *General Theory of Value*, and Urban's *Valuation, its Nature and Laws*, to name a few among many, are analyzing and explaining and classifying and grading the values that social man attaches or should attach to the conflicting and com-

[133] Beard, *Rise of American Civilization*, vol. 2, p. 589.

peting interests that enrich the fullness of his days.

Disagreement, not unnaturally, there is here, as in almost every science, at least in early stages. So far as value is merely subjective, one finds it hard to dispute about it just as one does in respect of taste.[135] Even in its subjective aspect, however, it is shaped in large degree by the pressure of external forces. Value, when seemingly the most personal, is, at least in part, a social product, the product of collective life. Some writers there are, indeed, such as Durkheim and Bouglé, who ascribe the leading rôle at all times to the creative power of society, no matter how subjective at first sight the estimate of worth may seem. Society, in Bouglé's words, "is essentially creator of ideals." [135] "By its properties, by the peculiar forces which emerge from the assembling of men, are to be explained the characteristics of those great magnets which are called values." [136] "Judgments of value have for function to formulate, not the natural properties of things, but the desires of men living in society." [137] Other writers, though giving heed to the motive forces that are external, lay greater emphasis upon forces that are individual and personal.[138] On the other hand, when the value to be appraised is value objectively considered, and particularly when the question is one of the preference

[135] Perry, *op. cit.*, sec. 12.
[135] Bouglé's *Evolution of Values*, Sellars' translation, p. 16.
[136] Bouglé, *op. cit.*, p. 16.
[137] Bouglé, *op. cit.*, p. 147.
[138] Urban, *op. cit.*; Perry, *op. cit.*

to be given to diverse or competing values, the social element emerges everywhere to fuller recognition. "A subjective value," we are told by Urban,[139] "is said to be actual, to have objective grounds, when it is in some sense continuous with, or convertible into, the social value." He argues, it is true, that this is not a final test, yet he concedes that for the most part subjective worths that are real have capacity of substitution with worths that are social, may be translated into terms of social objectivity.[140] For Bouglé, the social element is even more insistent. "Values," he tells us, adopting Durkheim's thought, "values are objective because *imperative*, and imperative because *collective*." [141]

There is significance in all this, it seems to me, for students of the judicial process. The judge who finds his moral value through his readings of the social mind, goes to the same source from which values generally are born, consults the same book that is spread open to us all. But a second point to be observed is this, that justice or moral value is only one value among many that must be appraised by the same method. Other values, not moral, values of expediency or of convenience or of economic or cultural advancement, a host of values that are not final, but merely means to others, are to be ascertained and assessed and equilibrated, the less sacrificed to the greater, all in subjection to like tests, the

139 *Op. cit.*, p. 388.
140 P. 408.
141 Bouglé, *op. cit.*, p. 16.

thought and the will and the desires of society as the
judge perceives and interprets them supplying the
measure and the scale. The aim of the jurist, we are
told by Pound, "at all times and in all the compromises and adjustments and reconciliations involved
in the legal order" should be "to give effect to as
much of the whole body of social interests as possible. . . . The compromises and adjustments that
will achieve the largest security of social interests
with the least sacrifice, must be sought through a
process of trial and error." [142] In all this, one must
beware of an axiology that is merely personal and
subjective. A judge is to give effect in general not to
his own scale of values, but to the scale of values
revealed to him in his readings of the social mind.
In particular he may not substitute his own reading
for one established by the legislature, acting within
constitutional limitations, through the pronouncements of a statute.[143] We may suspect that there have
been times when statutes have been condemned as
void under the influence of an axiology that failed in
this objective quality. Many are the times, however,
when there are no legislative pronouncements to
give direction to a judge's reading of the book of life
and manners. At those times, he must put himself as
best he can within the heart and mind of others, and
frame his estimate of values by the truth as thus
revealed. Objective tests may fail him, or may be so

[142] Pound, article "Jurisprudence," in the *History and Prospects
of the Social Sciences*, by Harry Elmer Barnes and others, p. 472.
[143] *Cf.* Cardozo, *The Growth of the Law*, p. 94.

confused as to bewilder. He must then look within himself.[144]

I have spoken of the process as one of compromise between stability and motion. Like the Aristotelian mean between extremes, the path of compromise will not be found by figuring the mean proportional as in an exercise in mathematics.[145] If two extremes present themselves as possible solutions of any given controversy, we do not reach the true solution by rejecting both extremes as certainly unacceptable, and seeking a middle course. There will be many situations in which one of the extremes will mark the course to be selected. What has been spoken of as a compromise is perhaps more accurately described as a concordance. A choice is arrived at by a balancing of interests, an appraisal of their value with reference to jural ends. It is a choice, even then, not between stability and unrestrained motion, but between stability and motion moderated and tempered by the immemorial traditions of a professional technique; it is erosion, not avulsion.[146]

Thinkers have complained with justice of the lack

[144] Cardozo, *The Nature of the Judicial Process*, p. 110; Brütt, *Die Kunst der Rechtsanwendung*, pp. 101, 139.

[145] *Cf.* Givler, ''Ethics,'' in the *History and Prospects of the Social Sciences*, by Harry Elmer Barnes and others, p. 487; Aristotle, *Nicomachean Ethics*, Book vi, Everyman's ed., p. 130.

[146] ''In thus showing that judges do and must make law, I do not, of course, wish to maintain that they are in no wise bound and can make any law they please. Every one who is engaged in making or creating something is limited by the rules of the process and the nature of the material.''—M. R. Cohen, ''Legal Theories and So-

of any formula whereby preference can be determined when values are conflicting. There is no common denominator to which it is possible to reduce them. In general we may say that where conflict exists, moral values are to be preferred to economic, and economic to aesthetic. Yet casuistry will discover overlappings and exceptions. We build skyscrapers, though smaller dwellings might be safer for the builders. We run railroads, though lives might be saved if we were satisfied to travel slowly. We experiment with airplanes, though pilots run the risk of death. Yet even in these cases, indifference to moral values is not as clear as it may seem upon the surface. Moral or cultural gains, cultural in a large sense, are often indirectly served, or will be in the years to come. The skyscraper gives economic opportunity to many who without it might feel the pinch of want. The railroad brings foods and medi-

cial Science,'' *The International Journal of Ethics*, July, 1915, pp. 476, 477.

We may say of law what Royce says of philosophy: ''Our common dependence upon the history of thought for all our reflective undertakings is unquestionable. Our best originality, if we ever get any originality, must spring from this very dependence. Doctrines of genuinely revolutionary significance are rare indeed in the history of speculation, and they ought to be. Of lesser surprises, of marvels, of beautifully novel insights, all the greater highways of speculation are full; and yet even most of the marvels are only such in so far as they are set off upon a very large background of the historically familiar. Only a very few times in the history of thought is the continuity of the evolution distinctly broken. The novelties are elsewhere only relative, and get their very value from the fact that they are so.'' — Royce, *The Spirit of Modern Philosophy*, Preface, p. vii.

cine and knowledge and many other forms of worth
when worth would evaporate with delay. The air-
plane has possibilities so many that fancy cannot
limit them. At all events a judge in his search for
objective estimates of value is helpless to establish
standards that will block the onward movement of
civilization as civilization is conceived of at any given
place or epoch. Individual predilections must yield
to a social pressure so resistless. Bouglé, indeed, insists that there can be found in what he calls "poly-
telism," [147] a reconciliation of apparent conflicts between one value and another. The same means has
capacity to serve a multiplicity of ends.[148] In the
present stage of the science of axiology, the picture
may seem to have an over-roseate hue. Yet the judge,
if he may not halt the march of civilization, may do
something at times to moderate its pace, to mitigate
its ruthless quality. The law will not prevent the
erection of skyscrapers. It may call for safety devices that will reduce the toll of lives. The law will
not prevent the operation of railroads. It may call
for signals and watchmen, and may raise or depress
the roadbed at the crossing of a highway. An adjustment may even be effected between economic
and aesthetic values. The landowner will not be compelled to forego every profitable use of his land, but
in some jurisdictions it is at least an open question
whether a restriction may not be placed upon the

[147] *Op. cit.*, p. 84.
[148] Pp. 84, 257.

construction of unsightly signs.[149] Here as so often it
is a question of degree. "The laws are silent amid
arms." The decree of a court will not stay the clash
of war, but it can halt the riot or the brawl or the
brutal and debasing prizefight.[150] Our function as
judges is not to transform civilization, but to regulate and order it. The book of life changes, and the
values revealed to us today may be different from
those that will be revealed to us tomorrow.

I said not long ago that the choice to be made is
not between stability and unrestrained motion, but
between stability and motion moderated and tempered by the immemorial traditions of a professional
technique. In the midst of these restraints the worker in the law is impressed ever and again with the
wealth of weapons in the legal armory. Repeatedly,
when one is hard beset, there are principles and precedents and analogies which may be pressed into the
service of justice if one has the perceiving eye to use
them. It is not unlike the divinations of the scientist.
His experiments must be made significant by the
flash of a luminous hypothesis. For the creative process in law, and indeed in science generally, has a
kinship to the creative process in art. Imagination,
whether you call it scientific or artistic, is for each
the faculty that creates. There are the successive

[149] See, however, Peo. *ex rel.* Wineburgh Adv. Co. *v.* Murphy, 1909,
195 N.Y. 126; and *cf.* Matter of Wulfsohn *v.* Burden, 1925, 241 N.Y.
288, 300, and Welch *v.* Swasey, 1909, 214 U.S. 91, 108; Baker, "Mu-
nicipal Aesthetics in the Law," *Ill. Law Rev.*, February, 1926.
[150] *In re* Debs., 1895, 158 U.S. 564.

stages of preparation, incubation and illumination described with so much insight by Graham Wallas in his analysis of the art of thought.[151] Learning is indeed necessary, but learning (to paraphrase what has been said of Keats) is the springboard by which imagination leaps to truth.[152] The law has its piercing intuitions, its tense, apocalyptic moments. We gather together our principles and precedents and analogies, even at times our fictions, and summon them to yield the energy that will best attain the jural end. If our wand has the divining touch, it will seldom knock in vain. So it is that the conclusion, however deliberate and labored, has often the aspect in the end of nothing but a lucky find.[153] "When I once asked the best administrator whom I knew," writes Mr. Wallas,[154] "how he formed his decisions, he laughed, and with the aid of letting out for the first time a guilty secret, said: 'Oh, I always decide by feeling. So and so always decides by calculation, and that is no good.' When, again, I asked an American judge, who is widely admired both for his skill and for his impartiality, how he and his fellows formed their conclusions, he also laughed, and said that he should be stoned in the street if it were known that, after listening with full consciousness to all the evidence, and following as carefully as he

[151] Wallas, *The Art of Thought*, pp. 80, 82, 94, 96.

[152] Lowell's *Life of Keats*, vol. 1, p. 477; *cf.* Wallas, *op. cit.*, p. 124.

[153] *Cf.* Cardozo, *The Growth of the Law*, pp. 92, 93.

[154] *Op. cit.*, p. 119.

could all the arguments, he waited until he 'felt' one
way or the other.'' He had elided the preparation
and the brooding, or at least had come to think of
them as processes of faint kinship with the state of
mind that followed. ''When the conclusion is there,''
says William James,[155] ''we have always forgotten
most of the steps preceding its attainment.''

One may think it strange that the material in the
legal storehouse has a capacity so varied to combine
and recombine in accordance with the forms of justice. The reason is not far to seek. A fruitful parent
of injustice is the tyranny of concepts.[156] They are
tyrants rather than servants when treated as real
existences and developed with merciless disregard of
consequences to the limit of their logic.[157] For the
most part we should deal with them as provisional
hypotheses to be reformulated and restrained when
they have an outcome in oppression or injustice.
But their empire, even when greatest, is never without limits. Here as elsewhere, tyranny breeds rebellion, and rebellion an emancipator. The concept,
overgrown, and swollen with excess of power, is
matched in the end by other concepts which put a
curb on its pretensions. This interplay of concepts

[155] *Principles of Psychology*, vol. 1, p. 260, quoted by Wallas, *op. cit.*, p. 96.

[156] Dickinson, *Administrative Justice and the Supremacy of Law in the United States*, p. 128; Cardozo, *Growth of the Law*, p. 100; Pound, *Interpretations of Legal History*, p. 119, *cf.* Hynes *v.* N. Y. Central R. R. Co., 1921, 231 N.Y. 229.

[157] *Cf.* Taine's definition of the classic spirit in *L'Ancien Regime*, p. 262, quoted by Wallas, p. 175.

has been developed with great clarity and power by Professor Dickinson of Princeton University in his recent book on *Administrative Justice and the Supremacy of Law in the United States.* "Almost every legal concept or principle," he writes,[158] "is found to be but the terminal of a scale which shades at its opposite extremity into another of exactly contrary tendency, and the line between the two oscillates from specific case to case according to the context. Thus the law of nuisance plays between the principle that every person is entitled to use his property for any purpose that he sees fit, and the opposing principle that every man is bound to use his property in such a manner as not to injure the property of his neighbor." Again the task of judging is found to be a choice between antithetical extremes. We seem to see the workings of an Hegelian philosophy of history whereby the tendency of every principle is to create its own antithesis or rival.[159] Concepts are useful, indeed indispensable, if kept within their place. We will press them quite a distance. Many a time they will give rise to rules which might just as well be the opposite were it not that in giving adherence to the opposite we should mutilate the symmetry of the legal order, the relation of its parts, its logical coherence.[160] These are values deeply imbedded in our law and its philosophy. "If we have not identities to work upon, we have at least resemblances;

[158] P. 135.

[159] Royce, *The Spirit of Modern Philosophy*, Hegel, pp. 212, 213.

[160] Dickinson, *op. cit.*, pp. 113, 119, 131, 141.

and on their basis can be constructed a legal system which, although far from attaining the inexorable and absolute certainty once thought possible, yet introduces a degree of beneficial order into a world that would be much worse without it."[161] A time comes, however, when the concepts carry us too far, or farther than we are ready to go with them, and behold, some other concept, with capacity to serve our needs, is waiting at the gate. "It is a peculiar virtue of our system of law,[162] that the process of inclusion and exclusion, so often employed in developing a rule, is not allowed to end with its enunciation, and that an expression in an opinion yields later to the impact of facts unforeseen."

The impact may come from a new fact. It may come from a changing estimate of policy or justice, which is to say the same thing in other words, since the current thought as to such matters is as much a fact as any other. What was ruled or next to ruled was well enough often according to the wisdom of its day. The light of a new day has set it forth as folly. "The difficulty is," I quote Professor Dickinson again,[163] "that the contemporary view of public policy shifts with successive generations, and what was once the goal of policy ceases in time to be so."[164] We must look around then for some avenue of re-

[161] Dickinson, *op. cit.*, p. 131.

[162] Brandeis, J., dissenting in Jaybird Mining Co. *v.* Weir, 1926, 271 U.S. 609.

[163] *Op. cit.*, p. 131.

[164] *Cf.* Brütt, *Die Kunst der Rechtsanwendung*, p. 183.

lease. "What is needed is not arbitrary discretion, but a rule for making exceptions — a rule for breaking a rule — and of such rules the law is of course full."[165] Sometimes the commitment to an outworn policy is too firm to be broken by the tools of the judicial process, at least without greater relaxation of the doctrine of *stare decisis* than has yet commended itself to judges.[166] This is why I have pleaded and still plead for a more intimate channel of connection between legislatures and courts, bodies which move today in stately isolation.[167] Even without this aid, much may still be done within the bounds of the traditional technique if only origins are thought of as subordinate to ends, and symmetry of formulas to symmetry of life.

There is nothing new in this notion of the subordination of legal concepts to expediency and justice, though as with many an old truth there is need to restate it now and again. What is new perhaps is the readiness to avow what has always been practiced, but practiced more or less intermittently, and at times with scant appreciation of the nature of the motive force.[168] Hesitant avowal has begotten conduct that is spasmodic and irregular: there has been a feeling, inarticulate to some extent, that the conduct was something to be deprecated, something calling for excuse. Instructive it is to observe the tri-

165 Dickinson, *op. cit.*, p. 139.
166 *Cf.* Wigmore, *Problems of Law*, pp. 79, 80.
167 "A Ministry of Justice," 35 *Harv. L.R.* 113.
168 Holmes, *The Common Law*, p. 1.

umphs of the *mores* in the face of this resistance. Let
me take such a concept as that of corporate personality. Holdsworth has some illuminating remarks
upon the development of that concept in the history
of English Law. He points out [169] that at first when
the idea of a corporation was new, "the lawyers
were inclined to lay more stress upon wide general
deductions" from the concept corporation. "Thus
they said that a corporation could not be seised to a
use, either because a corporation had no conscience,
or because the process of the court of Chancery could
not issue against it, or because it had no capacity to
take to another's use; and Blackstone stated that it
could not be a trustee. Because it could hold only in
its corporate capacity for the purpose of the corporation, it was said that a gift to a corporation and
another person or another corporation jointly, would
create, not a joint tenancy, but a tenancy in common;
for in such a case the two co-owners held in different
capacities." "No doubt," continues Holdsworth,
"these were legitimate deductions from the vague
and wide premises on which they were founded. But
they were found to be inconvenient in practice. And
so, on grounds of practical convenience, they have
been evaded or altered. Equity, contrary to Blackstone's dictum, found no difficulty in ruling that a
corporation could be trustee; and the legislature
has recently enabled a corporation to hold
jointly with another person or corporation. In

169 Holdsworth, *History of English Law*, vol. 9, pp. 51, 52.

fact, though these wide deductions drawn from the nature of corporate personality have called attention to salient incapacities of corporations as compared with natural persons, they have never been able to stand any severe strain. Practical convenience rather than theoretical considerations have, from the days of the Year Books onward, determined what activities are possible, and what are impossible to a corporation.'' There was fresh example of this truth when a metaphysical theory of corporate personality was found to be in conflict with the necessities of war. A corporation organized in England and subject to its law, but controlled by German shareholders, was held to be an enemy alien, when the question to be determined was its capacity to trade, though its metaphysical spirit was as English as any spirit could well be.[170] ''The limited liability,'' said Lord Halsbury,[171] ''was a very useful introduction into our system, and there was no reason why foreigners should not, while dealing honestly with us, partake of the benefit of that institution; but it seems to me too monstrous to suppose that for an unlawful (because, after the declaration of war, a hostile) purpose the forms of that institution should be used and enemies of the state while actually at war with us should be allowed to continue trading and actually to sue for their profits of trade in any English Court of Justice.''

[170] Daimler Co. *v.* Continental Tyre Co., 1916, 2 A.C. 307.
[171] P. 316.

III

The Equilibration of Interests — Cause and Effect — The Individual and Society — Liberty and Government

I would not seem to exaggerate the limits of fluidity either actual or desirable. The play of imagination upon the material in the legal store-room does not always evoke the spirit of change. There are times when it will yield the answer that rest should be preferred to motion. Fields there are in the domain of law where fundamental conceptions have been developed to their uttermost conclusions by the organon of logic. One finds this method of decision in much of the law of bills and notes. One finds it again in the law of real estate, though the presuppositions of the concepts, their logical implications, are not understandable unless the concepts are interpreted in the revealing light of history. One finds it again in one of the most baffling subjects of legal science, the so-called *Conflict of Law*. We deal there with the application of law in space. The walls of the compartments must be firm, the lines of demarcation plain, or there will be overlappings and encroachments with incongruities and clashes. In such circumstances, the finality of the rule is in itself a jural end. I do not mean that even in this sphere the judge who seeks to reach the heart of a concept, its inmost implications, may not find, when he has gained the core, that the concept is one with policy and justice. All this may be true, yet when I view the subject as a whole, I find logic to have been more remorseless here, more blind to final causes, than it has been in other fields. Very likely it has been too remorseless. If it has, that is beside my present point, which is not criticism, but description. I survey the legal scene, and report what I discover.

The tendency of principle and rule to conform to moral standards, which is a true avenue of growth for law, is not to be confounded with the suspension of all principle and rule and the substitution of sentiment or unregulated benevolence, which, pushed to an extreme, is the negation of all law. Every system of law has within it artificial devices which are deemed in the main and on the average to promote convenience or security or other forms of public good. These devices take the shape of rules or standards to which the individual though he be careless or ignorant, must at his peril conform. If they were to be abandoned by the law whenever they had been disregarded by the litigant affected, there would be no sense in making them. The individual must subscribe his will, and acknowledge its execution in the presence of witnesses. The gift *inter vivos* must be consummated by delivery, and will fail if it rest in mere executory intention.[172] The purchase by an infant of something not a necessity will be voidable though the infant is close to man's estate. The suit will fail unless begun within the term prescribed by law, though it be postponed but a day beyond. This does not mean that pressure is not exerted even in such cases to soften the rigor of undeviating conformity. At times the pressure is so great that courts have felt unable to withstand it. Witness the more or less insincere pretexts by which courts of equity avoid at times the enforcement of the statute of frauds upon some theory of part performance or of the breach of a constructive trust. This instance is the more noteworthy because there the court has struggled against the compulsion of a statute. The fact remains, however, that law, like social institutions generally, attains its aim as a device for promoting order and reducing waste at the price of occasional hardship when its mandate is disregarded or fogotten.[178] This without more does not defeat its binding force. There may be some clearing and pruning even then. There will be no tearing up of roots. The time may come, however, when hardship is so acute and general that the good of the device, submerged in the evil, is forgotten and invisible. The rule survives, if at all, as

172 F. L. & T. Co. *v.* Windthrop, 238 N.Y. 477.

173 Stammler, "Fundamental Tendencies in Modern Jurisprudence," 21 *Mich. L.R.* 873; also Wu, appendix to Stammler's *Theory of Justice*, Modern Legal Phil. Series, p. 581; Cardozo, *Nature of the Judicial Process*, p. 138.

nothing more than a vestigial relic.[174] When this stage arrives, its days of life are numbered.

Two cases recently determined in my own court will illustrate my thought. The rule was settled at common law that an undisclosed principal might not be held to liability upon a contract which had been executed under seal. Much of the law as to seals has small relation in society as now organized to present-day realities. The question came up whether we would adhere to the rule that I have mentioned, or hold it to have faded away with the fading significance of seals. The decision was that the old rule would be enforced.[175] Precedents of recent date made departure difficult if *stare decisis* was not to be abandoned altogether, but there were other and deeper grounds of policy. Contracts had been made and transactions closed on the faith of the law as it had been theretofore declared. Men had taken title in the names of "dummies," and through them executed deeds and mortgages with the understanding, shared by the covenantees, that liability on the covenant would be confined to the apparent principal. They had done this honestly and without concealment. Something might be said, too, in favor of the social utility of a device by which the liability of the apparent principal could be substituted without elaborate forms for the liability of another back of him who was to reap the profits of the transaction. The law has like devices for limiting liability in other

---

174 *Cf.* Salmond, *Jurisprudence*, pp. 167, 168.

175 Crowley *v.* Lewis, 1924, 239 N.Y. 264.

situations, as, *e.g.*, in joint stock associations, corporations, and limited partnerships. In any event
retrospective change would be unjust. The evil, if it
was one, was to be eradicated by statute.

Not long after, there came another case in which
the ancient law of seals was again the controlling
factor.[176] The question then was whether we would
adhere to the old rule that a parol contract was ineffective to modify a contract under seal. We had
already abandoned this rule where the later contract, though parol, had been followed by performance. We had even intimated that it ought
to be abandoned though the later contract was executory.[177] There was authority for such a holding in
other jurisdictions.[178] When the question came before
us squarely, we held the other way, though by a
closely divided vote. I do not challenge the learning
and power of the majority opinion. There is no gain-
saying its conclusion if the judicial function is merely static. What seemed to be a division as to the law
was in truth a difference of philosophy. Conceiving
the judicial function as dynamic, I am still impressed
with the conviction that there was here a fitting opportunity to uproot an ancient evil. It is safe to say
that the later contract was not signed in the belief
that the omission of a seal had reduced it to an
empty form. If there was any such reservation in the
mind of one of the signers, he was dealing unfairly

176 Cammack *v.* Slattery & Bros., Inc., 1925, 241 N.Y. 39.
177 Harris *v.* Shorall, 230 N.Y. 343.
178 *Williston on Contracts*, vol. 3, sec. 1836.

by the other signer when he made delivery of the instrument as of something authentic and effective. But the truth is, of course, that he had no such reservation. The suggestion that there was need of a seal was transparently an afterthought, a pretext for the avoidance of a burdensome engagement. The displacement of the ancient rule would have done violence to no interest that was worthy of protection. It would have kept the movement of the law in pace with the movement of events. The displacement would not even have been attended by the shock of surprise, for earlier decisions had shown forth the absurdity of the rule and predicted in guarded terms that it would soon be decently interred with all the rites appropriate to venerable but departed dogma. Here, I venture to believe, is a situation in which stability was unwisely chosen to the sacrifice of progress. Let us hope that through the aid of statute a better justice will prevail.

In problems such as these, the need is fairly obvious for a balancing of social interests and a choice proportioned to the value. One is surprised at every turn to find that the same need is present, lurking beneath the surface, when other processes and methods, at least upon a hasty view, might seem predominant or perhaps exclusive. Take such a legal concept as the familiar one of negligence. Involved at every turn is the equilibration of social interests, moral and economic. Negligence as a term of legal art is, strictly speaking, a misnomer, for negligence connotes to the ordinary man the notion of lack of care, and yet one can be negligent in the view of the law though one has taken what one has supposed to be extraordinary care, and not negligent though one has taken no care at all.[179] Moreover, one can deliberately choose to be indifferent to the greatest peril, and yet avoid the charge of negligence for all one's scorn of prudence.[180]

Two factors, both social, contribute to the paradox. The first is the conception of the "reasonable man," the man who conforms in conduct to the common standards of society. If the individual falls short of the standards of the group, he does so at his peril. He must then answer for his negligence though his attention never flagged. Enough that a reasonable man would have appreciated the peril which because of stupidity or ignorance may have been hidden to the actor. The standard may be different for infants. It may be different also for those whose ignorance or stupidity is carried to such a point as to put them in the class of the abnormal, — the insane or the defective, — though as to this the law is still unsettled.[181] On the other hand, if one acts at one's peril when one falls below the common

179 Edgerton, "Negligence, Inadvertence and Indifference," 39 *Harv. L.R.* 849.

180 Wagner *v.* Int. Ry. Co., 232 N.Y. 176.

181 Bohlen, *Studies in the Law of Torts*, "Liability in Tort of Infants and Insane Persons," p. 543; Seavey, "Negligence; Subjective or Objective," 41 *Harvard L.R.* 1; see, however, Williams *v.* Hays, 143 N.Y. 442; 157 N.Y. 541; O'Connor *v.* Hickey, Mass., 156 N.E. Rep. 838.

standard, one may have protection at the other extreme; one may not need to go beyond it. There may be occasions when an individual charged with negligence has taken no care at all or at all events very little, and yet by luck has conformed in overt act to the standard of conduct exacted of the diligent. In such a case, his mere subjective delinquency, the mere negligence of his thought, will not avail without more to put liability upon him.[182] Very likely the law has not been wholly consistent in this field any more than it has been in others. The standard of common care as measured by the conduct of a reasonable man is at times the expression of a minimum of duty rather than a maximum. If the individual has special skill or opportunities for knowledge, he may be required to do whatever a reasonable man would do if equally favored by nature and occasion.[183] By and large, however, with whatever allowance may be made for deviation or exception, the test of liability is external and objective.

There is, however, a second factor that contributes to the paradox. I may call it the calculus of interests. The measure of care imputed to that standardized being, the reasonable man, is one dependent upon the value of the interests involved. As to this I have learned much from Professor Bohlen, a great master of the law of Torts. The law measures the risks that a man may legitimately take by measuring the value

[182] Edgerton, *supra*; Seavey, *supra*.
[183] Seavey, *supra*.

of the interests furthered by his conduct. I may accumulate explosives for the purpose of doing some work of construction that is important for mankind when I should be culpably reckless in accumulating them for pleasure or caprice. I may risk my life by plunging into a turbulent ocean to save a drowning man when I should be culpably reckless if I were to make the plunge for sport or mere bravado. Inquiries that seem at the first glance the most simple and unitary — was this or that conduct negligent or the opposite? — turn out in the end to be multiple and complex. Back of the answers is a measurement of interests, a balancing of values, an appeal to the experience and sentiments and moral and economic judgments of the community, the group, the trade. Of course, some of these valuations become standardized with the lapse of years, and thus instantaneous or, as it were, intuitive. We know at once that it is negligence to drive at breakneck pace through a crowded street, with children playing in the centre, at least where the motive of the drive is the mere pleasure of the race. On the other hand, a judgment even so obvious as this yields quickly to the pressure of new facts with new social implications. We assign a different value to the movement of the fire engine or the ambulance. Constant and inevitable, even when half concealed, is the relation between the legality of the act and its value to society. We are balancing and compromising and adjusting every moment that we judge.

The endless variety of the process is indeed a source of never-ceasing wonder. One would suppose after all these centuries of judging that the frontier would have vanished, that there would no longer be unsettled soil, no longer nebulae and star dust, but only peopled worlds. Yet in truth it is not so. There are topics where the law is still unformed and void. Some hint or premonition of coming shapes and moulds, it betrays amid the flux, yet it is so amorphous, so indeterminate, that formulation, if attempted, would be the prophecy of what is to be rather than the statement of what is. Matter, in Spencer's famous, if obsolete, definition of the process of evolution, "passes from an indefinite, incoherent homogeneity to a definite, coherent heterogeneity." So it is with the growth of law. Every topic is coherent with reference to some incoherence that is past, and incoherent with reference to some coherence yet to be. I am struck by this, from day to day, in the course of my judicial work. I am struck by it again when following the work of the American Law Institute in the restatement of the law. One cannot have a part, however humble, in the execution of that project without a mounting sense of wonder that with all our centuries of common law development, with all our multitudinous courts and still more multitudinous decisions, there are so many questions, elementary in the sense of being primary and basic, that remain unsettled even now. If they were propounded to you

suddenly, you would say that of course there must
be authorities in abundance for anything so fundamental. You might feel some pricks of conscience at
your own ignorance in being unable to repeat the
proper answer out of hand. You would have your
self-respect restored in some degree if you came to
survey the field, and found that the answer, if there
was any, was at best uncertain and obscure. I have
noticed this particularly in connection with the law
of torts. Rights and privileges at the root, it would
seem, of life in civilized society, are discovered to
be involved in doubt. One wonders how one has attained maturity without getting oneself in trouble
when one has been so uncertain all along of the
things that one might do in affairs of primary concern. Take such fundamental privileges or claims of
privilege as these — the privilege to employ force
against another who threatens one with bodily harm;
the privilege to employ force to effect a recaption of
chattels taken from one's custody; the privilege to
employ force to effect an entry upon land. It is aston-
ishing how obscure and confused are the pronouncements upon these fundamental claims of right. What
is certain is that the gaps in the system will be filled,
and filled with ever-growing consciousness of the implications of the process, by a balancing of social interests, an estimate of social values, a reading of the
social mind.

I have no thought to underrate the tribulations of
the process. They have been known these many years.

From the press of Cambridge University there has come of recent days a translation by an English scholar [184] of the manual of Roman Law known as the Ecloga. Leo III and Constantine V, Roman Emperors, published it at Constantinople in 726. They ordered a group of scholars to render into Greek parts of the Institutes, the Digests, the Code and the Novels of "the great Justinian," improving his commands, however, "in the direction of humanity." To the judges of the empire and to all who aspired to judicial office, the Emperors said this: "Let those, and those only, who participate in sense and reason, and know clearly what true justice is, exercise straight vision in their judgments, and without passion apportion to each his deserts." Perhaps with all my talk about the compromise between antithetical extremes, I have not improved a great deal upon this formula of the Byzantine Emperors, though 1200 years have passed between their effort and my own.

I suspect that the Emperors found it easier to give their advice than the judges did to follow it. Certain it is, at all events, that the contrast between exhortation and obedience has not lessened with the years. I question whether many of you appreciate the misgivings that afflict a judge's mind when he has done the best he can, and handed down his judgment to be enshrined in the reports. Some, of course, are blessed with a spirit more robust. In a memoir

[184] Edwin Hanson Freshfield.

of the Earl of Halsbury, Lord Birkenhead speaks of
"his stubborn and unconquerable pertinacity of view
alike in the legal and political fields." "I do not recall," says his biographer, "that he ever admitted
that he had been wrong in either. Nor do I believe
that he ever thought so."[185] My acquaintance with
judges inclines me to the view that such self-suffi-
ciency is rare, though perhaps to some extent I am
jumping to the conclusion that they survey the scene
of life through lenses of the same power that are
fitted to my eyes. Yet the travail with all its pangs is
not peculiar to the bench. The worker in other fields
of intellectual effort shares it with the judge. I pick
up at random a book by a philosopher and man of
letters. It tells of his perturbed and unhappy state
of mind when he goes over his old writings.[186] He is
tempted, he says, to change them in new editions, and
then he argues, that, if he does, some of his readers
may prefer the first edition to the second, and perhaps, living a decade longer, he may come to a like
preference himself. That is my state of mind, and
there is my consolation. I go over the old opinions,
and wonder whether they are right, and then I say
to myself that if I had written the other way, I should
be just as doubtful as before. I suppose the defeated
counsel will be a little less philosophical about the
matter than I have tried to be, and will wish that I
had hazarded the experiment of a change, but then I

[185] Birkenhead, *Fourteen English Judges*, p. 360.
[186] Santayana, Preface to the second edition of the *Life of Reason.*

reflect that his adversary would wish otherwise, and so the *chose jugée* abides. I see no remedy for such agonies, though men have sought for it these many years. Bertrand Russell reminds us in his paper on "Mathematics and Metaphysics," [187] that "two hundred years ago, the philosopher Leibnitz conceived a plan for an art of formal reasoning from which he hoped for a solution of all problems and an end to all disputes. If controversies arose, there would be no more need of disputation between two philosophers than between two accountants, for it would suffice for them to take their pens in their hands, sit down at their tables, and say to each other, let us calculate." If only Leibnitz's dream could be realized in the law! In the meanwhile, we must be content to stumble along the path, and offer up thanksgivings that we have not fallen into the pit.

I have spoken of the misgivings that afflict a judge's mind. Yet I would not leave you with the impression that inevitably and always they survive the declaration of the judgment. The curious thing is that sometimes in the hardest cases, in cases where the misgivings have been greatest at the beginning, they are finally extinguished, and extinguished most completely. I have gone through periods of uncertainty so great, that I have sometimes said to myself, "I shall never be able to vote in this case either one way or the other." Then, suddenly, the fog has lifted. I have reached a stage of mental peace. I know

[187] *Mysticism and Logic*, p. 79.

in a vague way that there is doubt whether my conclusion is right. I must needs admit the doubt in view of the travail that I suffered before landing at the haven. I cannot quarrel with any one who refuses to go along with me; and yet, for me, however it may be for others, the judgment reached with so much pain has become the only possible conclusion, the antecedent doubts merged, and finally extinguished, in the calmness of conviction. I have little question that these recurrent stages of agitation and serenity are the common experience of other toilers in fields of intellectual effort. All the more precious is the final peace for the storm that went before it. A highly developed machine has been turned over to our keeping, a machine with intricate cogs and weights and balances, the work of many minds. Small wonder that we lie awake at nights in fear that some new apprentice, who was supposed to lubricate the joints, may turn out in the end to be either a bungler or an enemy, and set the whole appliance out of gear.

As we take leave of the antithesis of rest and motion and its solution in the law, our dominant impression must be one of compromise, of adjustment, of a pragmatic adaptation of means to ends, of the relativity of legal truths. The same principle of relativity is at the root of the treatment in law of another age-long antithesis, the antithesis of cause and effect. The law has its problems of causation. It must trace events to causes, or say with Hume that there is no cause, but only juxta-position or succession.

If it recognizes causation, as it does, it must determine which antecedent shall be deemed to be the jural cause, the antecedent to be selected from an infinite series of antecedents as big with the event. We are told very often that the law concerns itself with proximate causes and no others. The statement is almost meaningless, or rather, to the extent that on the surface it has meaning, it is far away from truth. Sometimes in the search for the jural cause, the law stops close to the event, but sometimes and often, it goes many stages back. The principle of the relativity of causation tells us that its methods could not well be different. "Cause," says Lord Haldane in his book, *The Reign of Relativity*,[188] "is a very indefinite expression. Externality to the effect is of its essence, but its meaning is relative in all cases to the subject-matter. For the housemaid the cause of the fire is the match she lights and applies. For the physicist the cause of the fire is the conversion of potential into kinetic energy, through the combination of carbon atoms with those of oxygen and the formation of oxides in the shape of gases which become progressively oxidized. For the judge who is trying a case of arson it is the wicked action of the prisoner in the dock. In each case there is a different field of inquiry, determined from a different standpoint. But no such field is even approximately exhaustive. The complete cause, if it could be found, would extend to the entire ground of the phenomenon

[188] Pp. 125, 126.

that had to be explained, and this ground would reach, not only to the whole of the world, but the entirety of the universe. More than this: if the ground could be completely stated it would be indistinguishable from the effect itself, including, as it would do, the whole of the conditions of existence. Thus we see that when we speak of the cause of an event we are only picking out what is relevant to the standpoint of a special inquiry, and is determined in its scope by the particular concept which our purpose makes us have in view.'' [189]

Here is the key to the juridical treatment of the problems of causation. We pick out the cause which in our judgment ought to be treated as the dominant one with reference, not merely to the event itself, but to the jural consequences that ought to attach to the event. There is an opinion by Lord Shaw in the English House of Lords in which he refers to the common figure of speech whereby a succession of causes is represented as a chain. He reminds us that the figure, though convenient, is inadequate. ''Causation,'' he says, ''is not a chain, but a net. At each point, influences, forces, events, precedent and simultaneous meet, and the radiation from each point extends infinitely.'' [190] From this complex web the law picks out now this cause and now that one. Thus the same event may have one jural cause when it is considered as giving rise to a cause of action upon

[189] *Cf.* Kohler, *Phil. of Law*, 12 Modern Legal Phil. Series, p. 35.
[190] Leland Shipping Co. *v.* Norwich Fire Ins. Society, *L.R.* 1918 A.C. 350, 369.

contract, and another when it is considered as giving rise to a cause of action for a tort. The law accepts or rejects one or another as it measures its own ends and the social benefits or evils of rejection or acceptance.

A case will point my meaning. A fire occurred at Big Tom, New Jersey. The fire exploded dynamite. The explosion by its vibrations caused damage to a vessel standing out in the river half a mile away. A policy of insurance secured the owner of the vessel against loss proximately caused by fire. The court assumed that by the law in most jurisdictions the fire would be the jural cause if the action were in tort against a wrongdoer who had negligently spread the flames. Indisputably it would if he had acted with intent to cause the very damage that resulted. On the other hand, the court refused to find that the fire was the jural cause within the meaning of the contract.[191]

The reasoning that led to this conclusion is in close approach to Lord Haldane's, though rendition of the judgment preceded by some years the publication of his book. "In last analysis," we said, "it is something in the minds of men, in the will of the contracting parties, and not merely in the physical bond of union between events, which solves, at least for the jurist, this problem of causation. In all this, there is nothing anomalous. Everything in nature is cause and effect by turns. For the physicist, one thing is the cause; for the jurist, another. Even for the jurist,

[191] Bird *v.* Ins. Co., 1918, 224 N.Y. 47.

the same cause is alternately proximate and remote
as the parties choose to view it. A policy provides
that the insurer shall not be liable for damage caused
by the explosion of a boiler. The explosion causes a
fire. If it were not for the exception in the policy, the
fire would be the proximate cause of the loss and the
explosion the remote one. By force of the contract,
the explosion becomes proximate.[192] A collision oc-
curs at sea and fire supervenes. The fire may be the
proximate cause and the collision the remote one for
the purpose of an action on the policy. The collision
remains proximate for the purpose of suit against
the colliding vessel.[193] There is nothing absolute in
the legal estimate of causation. Proximity and re-
moteness are relative and changing concepts.''[194]
We see then why so much of the discussion of
proximate cause in case and in commentary is mysti-
fying and futile. There is a striving to give absolute
validity to doctrines that must be conceived and
stated in terms of relativity. No doubt, the tests propounded have value and significance. The difficulty in
applying them, however, has its origin in the failure
to remember that they are in truth, not tests, but
clews. They help to guide the judgment in laying emphasis upon one cause or another among the many

[192] St. John *v.* Am. Mut. F. & M. Ins. Co., 1854, 11 N.Y. 516; Ins.
Co. *v.* Tweed, 1868, 7 Wall. 44.

[193] N. Y. & B. D. Ex. Co. *v.* Traders' & M. Ins. Co., 132 Mass., 377,
382.

[194] Bird *v.* Ins. Co., *supra*, at pp. 54, 55; Kerr S. S. Co. *v.* Radio
Corp., 1927, 245 N.Y. 284, 290.

that are secreted in the tangles of the web.[195] I find the same idea prefigured in an illuminating discussion by Professor Edgerton of the meaning of legal cause. I do not say that I would follow him in all his conclusions as to the relative function of judge and jury. For present purposes it is enough to mark the discernment and understanding with which he penetrates to the heart and essence of the problem. "A legal cause," he says,[196] "is a justly-attachable cause; (or) a legal consequence is a justly-attachable consequence; (or) a legal cause is a cause which stands in such a relation to its consequence that it is just to give legal effect to the relation; meaning by 'just,' not merely fair as between the parties, but socially advantageous, as serving the most important of the competing individual and social interests involved." [197] The truth which the law seeks in tracing events to causes is truth pragmatically envisaged, truth relative to jural ends.

From rest and motion, cause and effect, I pass to other opposites, the one and the many, the individual and the group, the group and the community, liberty and government.

The individual person is the atom in the social structure. The atom does not exist in isolation. It

[195] *Cf.* James Angell McLaughlin, "Proximate Cause," 39 *Harvard L.R.* 149; Henry W. Edgerton, "Legal Cause," 72 *Univ. of Penn. L.R.* 211, 343; Joseph H. Beale, "The Proximate Consequences of an Act," 83 *H.L.R.* 633.

[196] 72 *Univ. of Penn. L.R.* 348.

[197] *Cf.* Bohlen, "Mixed Questions of Law and Facts," 72 *Univ. of Penn. L.R.* 120; Studies in the Law of Torts, p. 601.

combines with other atoms in response to a persistent instinct. The force or tendency by which the individual is moved to associate with others is known by the name of syngenism.[198] To syngenism, we owe the group in all its phases, at the lowest range the family, at the uppermost the state. The group is not a constant quantity. It is subject to Protean changes. We have, along with others, the clan, the church, the club, the guild, each evoking loyalties, but loyalties varying in intensity at different times and places. There are attractions and repulsions between one individual and another, between individuals and groups, and finally between groups themselves. Energies must be released and energies must be curbed. The reconciliation of these opposites is one of the outstanding problems of the law; it is the problem of liberty and government.

The state exists to subordinate to law, and thereby to order and coherence, the rivalries and struggles of its component groups and individuals. It is thus, in the words of Small [199] ''a union of disunions, a conciliation of conflicts, a harmony of discords. There is combination and there is severance; there is the setting of bonds and there is the loosening of bonds; there is conservation and there is change; there is a 'stereotyping principle' and there is an 'innovating principle'.'' [200] For every strophe an antistrophe.

[198] Barnes, *Sociology and Political Theory*, p. 53.
[199] *General Sociology*, p. 252; *cf.* Barnes, *op. cit.*, p. 33.
[200] Small, *op. cit.*, p. 257.

The metronome of the law prescribes the interval between them.

One of the strange things about syngenism is that in creating the group, it recreates or modifies the individual. The individual in the group — in the trade union or the political party or the state — is not the same as the individual out of the group. His will has been transfigured by association with the wills of others. This does not mean that there is a mystical common will which belongs to the group as a person separate from its members. All that it means is that the wills of individuals like their habits and desires are modified by the interaction between mind and mind. The social mind is indeed the sum of the individual minds, but it is the sum of them when associated, and not their sum when dissevered. Thus interpreted Rousseau's *volonté générale* corresponds to a deep truth. Press it to greater lengths, and it is turned into a confusing fiction. This, I think, at least among Anglo-American students of the social sciences, is today the dominant conception of the mental life of groups. Thus Laski in his *Grammar of Politics*: [201] ''Corporate personality and the will that it embodies, is real in the sense that it makes those upon whom it acts different from what they were before. But it remains different from the uniqueness which makes me separate from the rest of the universe. The unity of England is in the historic tradition which orientates a vast number of wills in a

[201] P. 32.

similar direction; it is not in some mystic super-will
built from their fusion." So Hobhouse in his *Social
Evolution and Political Theory*: [202] "What has been
said may be sufficient to show that when we speak of
social thought, social will or, more generally, of
social mind we neither imply a mystical psychic unity nor a fully achieved consciousness of the social
life on the part of the component members of society.
Such a consciousness is in fact a developed product
of the social mind, but its presence is not to be assumed wherever the term 'social mind' is used. This
term is simply an expression for the mass of ideas
operative in a society, communicable from man to
man, and serving to direct the thoughts and actions
of individuals." And again,[203] "By the social mind,
then, we mean not necessarily a unity pervading
any given society as a whole, but a tissue of operative psychological forces which in their higher de-
velopments crystallize into unity within unity, and
into organism operating upon organism. We mean
something essentially of psychological character that
arises from the operations of masses of men, and
molds and is in turn remolded by the operation of
masses of men; which has no existence except in the
minds of men, and yet is never fully realized in the
mind of any one man; which depends on the social
relations between man and man, but takes full cog-
nizance of the relation only in the higher stages of

[202] P. 96.
[203] P. 97.

its development.'' The same thought is happily stated by Dr. Seligman: [204] ''Thus the group is neither an organism nor a phantom. It is an entity which, although composed of individuals, is not only abstractly but concretely distinct from the individuals concerned as non-group members. In short, although the group is created by individuals, it, in part at least, recreates the individual. It is the expression of the way in which separate wants are transmuted into common wants; it is the realization of the method by which the satisfactions of the individual become possible only through, and in unison with, the satisfactions of other individuals; it is the embodiment of the process by which the ever-present and ineradicable self-interest of human beings is slowly permeated by the broader feeling which in the finest individuals grows into loyalty and unselfishness.'' [205]

It would carry me too far afield if I were to consider at any length the character of the group as a juristic person, though the problem is not unrelated to the antitheses of the law, seeing that it is a phase of the eternal riddle of nominalism and realism, phenomenon and noumenon, appearance and reality. In Anglo-American Law, the so-called concession theory was long supposed to be the accepted doctrine.

[204] ''The Social Theory of Fiscal Science,'' 41 *Pol. Sci. Q.* 210.

[205] *Cf.* Ernest Barker, *Political Thought from Herbert Spencer to the Present Day*, Home University Library, p. 175; MacIver, *Community*, pp. 78, 79; Small, *General Sociology*, p. 142; Young, *Social Psychology in History and Prospects of the Social Sciences*, by H. E. Barnes and others, p. 156.

The group as a juristic person does not come into
being, according to this theory, until the state by
appointed organs has declared that he shall live.
"Corporate life and form," says Holdsworth,[206]
"cannot exist without the permission of the state,
express, presumed or implied." [207] There are indeed
distinguished students of jurisprudence who are
sponsors for an opposing theory.[208] The group in
their view is a "real living thing," quite independent of any permission to exist as an incorporated
person that may have been given by the state.[209] I
may digress long enough to point out that this real
living thing has made some curious breaches only
lately in the doctrine held for orthodox. He has suc-
ceeded very recently in causing his existence to be
recognized in advance of official declaration, though
he has made his entrance upon the legal scene in a
rather shame-faced sort of way, and, as it were, by
the back door. The general rule may still be that corporate personality is a legislative gift rather than a

206 *History of English Law,* vol. 9, p. 48.

207 *Cf.* Henderson, *Foreign Corporations in American Constitutional Law,* pp. 165, 167; Kohler, *Phil. of Law,* 12 Modern Legal
Phil. Series, p. 68.

208 Consult Holdsworth, *op. cit.,* vol. 9, p. 48; Dewey, "The His-
toric Background of Corporate Legal Personality," 35 *Yale L.J.,* p.
655; Maitland, Introduction to Gierke's *Political Theories of Middle
Age;* Barker, *Political Thought from Spencer to Today,* pp. 175-180;
Laski, "The Personality of Associations," 29 *H.L.R.* 404; Borchard,
"Government Responsibility in Tort," 36 *Yale L.J.* 757, 774; Gel-
dart, *Legal Personality;* Bijur, J., in F. L. & T. Co. *v.* Pierson, 130
Misc. N.Y. 11.

209 Holdsworth, vol. 9, p. 47.

quality inherent in the very nature of a group. It seems, however, that at times even in our law a group has a solidarity so obvious as to evoke judicial recognition of its corporate or quasi-corporate existence, though no charter to act as a corporation has been either given or desired.[210] By the judgment of the Supreme Court of the United States in United Workers of America *v.* Coronado Coal Co., 259 U.S. 344, 385, 387, 388, an unincorporated trade union was held subject to suit as a *persona ficta*.[211] The summary pronouncement of the opinion would give scant notice to the uninformed that behind it lay an age-long controversy and a prolific legal literature. Our English brethren have gone farther. By a recent ruling of the Judicial Committee of the Privy Council,[212] a wooden idol worshipped in India as divine, was recognized as a *persona* in England, since it was so recognized in India. Accordingly lest its rights might be infringed, the judgment was reversed, and a guardian was appointed to represent the sacred effigy. Here the quality of personality was attributed not to a man or an aggregate of men, but to a thing confessedly inanimate. Analogies may be found in the corporate personality of the *fiscus* long familiar to European law,[213] and again in the personality of

[210] *Cf.* MacIver, *The Modern State*, p. 475.

[211] *Cf.* Taff Vale Ry. Co. *v.* A. S. R. S., 1901, A.C. 426.

[212] Mulleck *v.* Mulleck, 1925, *L.R.*, 52 Ind. App. 245; "The Personality of an Idol," P. W. Duff, 3 *Cambridge L.J.* 42.

[213] Jones, "The Early History of the Fiscus," 43 *L.Q.R.* 499, 502; M. R. Cohen, "Communal Ghosts and Other Perils in Social Phil-

the "Stiftung" or foundation.[214] A remote analogy
may be found in the recognition of foreign corporations as persons, capable, under many decisions, of
suing and being sued in our courts, if such capacity
is theirs in the jurisdiction of the domicile. There is
no occasion at this time to approve or to condemn
these extensions of the notion of corporate personality. Some can be explained as instances of the application of "comity" or some principle akin thereto
in accordance with established doctrines of private
international law.[215] Others suggest a developing
rapprochement between jurisprudence and sociology
in the decisions of our courts. We are taking over
social concepts and setting the imprimatur of the law
upon them.

I put aside, however, for the time as foreign to
my major theme the fascinating subject of the reality
of corporate personality. Reality at least there is in
the sense that among the phenomena of society are
groups, not haphazard and occasional, but persistent
and pervasive, which change the needs and the interests of the individuals within them. The law could
not ignore this if it would, for if the groups are
figured as concentric circles, the outer one is the

osophy," vol. 16, *Journal Philosophy, Psychology and Scientific Method,* 679, 680.

214 Saleilles, *La Personalité Juridique, passim;* Roguin, *La Règle
de Droit,* vol. 2, pp. 434, 460, *et seq.;* Gray, *Nature and Sources of
Law,* sections 137-140; Wise's *Outlines of Jurisprudence,* 4th ed. by
Oliver, p. 49.

215 Young, "The Legal Personality of a Foreign Corporation,"
22 *L.Q.R.* 178, 187.

state itself. When therefore the state by its judges attempts to mark the respective limits of liberty and government, it must draw the line in such a way that the individual and the group, and the life appropriate to each, may have scope and opportunity for harmonious development. The location of this line is the overshadowing problem of liberty and law.

Liberty as a legal concept contains an underlying paradox. Liberty in the most literal sense is the negation of law, for law is restraint, and the absence of restraint is anarchy. On the other hand, anarchy by destroying restraint would leave liberty the exclusive possession of the strong or the unscrupulous. "This is a world of compensation," said Lincoln,[216] "and he who would be no slave must consent to have no slave." So once more we face a paradox.

The paradox was long ago perceived by Locke who gave expression to it in terms that have not been bettered since his day.[217] "For law in its true notion," he said, "is not so much the limitation as the direction of a free and intelligent agent to his proper interest, and prescribes no farther than is for the general good of those under that law. . . . That ill deserves the name of confinement which hedges us in only from bogs and precipices. So that however it may be mistaken, the end of law is not to abolish or restrain, but to preserve and enlarge freedom. For in all the states of created beings, capable of laws,

[216] Sandburg's *Life of Lincoln*, vol. 2, p. 182.
[217] *Treatises on Civil Government*, book 2, sec. 57.

where there is no law there is no freedom. For liberty is to be free from restraint and violence from others, which cannot be where there is no law; and is not, as we are told, 'liberty for every man to do what he lists.' For who could be free, when every other man's humour might domineer over him? But a liberty to dispose and order freely as he lists his person, actions, possessions, and his whole property within the allowance of those laws under which he is, and therein not to be subject to the arbitrary will of another, but freely follow his own." Modern research in social science has amplified the thought of Locke, but without changing its essentials.

"If liberty is a social conception," says Hobhouse,[218] "there can be no liberty without social restraint. For any one person, indeed, there might be a maximum of liberty if all social restraints were removed. Where physical strength alone prevails the strongest man has unlimited liberty to do what he likes with the weaker; but clearly the greater the freedom of the strong man, the less the freedom of the weaker. What we mean by liberty as a social conception is a right to be shared by all members of society, and very little consideration suffices to show that, in the absence of restraints enforced on or accepted by all members of a society, the liberty of some must involve the oppression of others. . . . Excess of liberty contradicts itself. In short there is no

[218] *Social Evolution and Political Theory,* p. 189.

such thing; there is only liberty for one and restraint for another.'' [219]

Is there then no path of compromise except such as may be marked by the opportunism of the hour? We find in state and national constitutions a pledge of individual liberty. By common consent this means at least immunity from slavery or serfdom. In so far as it seems to promise more, are we restricted to a choice between a rhetorical flourish and a canonization of what is? Is there no criterion of rationality to enlighten decision with the inspiration of a principle?

In delimiting the field of liberty, courts have professed for the most part to go about their work empirically and have rather prided themselves on doing so. They have said, we will not define due process of law. We will leave it to be ''pricked out'' by a process of inclusion and exclusion in individual cases. [220] That was to play safely, and very likely at the beginning to play wisely. The question is how long we are to be satisfied with a series of *ad hoc* conclusions. It is all very well to go on pricking the lines, but the time must come when we shall do prudently to look them over, and see whether they make a pattern or a medley of scraps and patches. I do not suggest that political or social science has formulated a conception of liberty so precise and accurate that, applied as a

[219] *Cf.* the same author's *Liberalism*, Home University Library, pp. 23, 139, 140, 144, 145.

[220] Davidson *v.* New Orleans, 1877, 96 U.S. 97, 104; *cf.* Village of Euclid *v.* Ambler Realty Co., 1926, 272 U.S. 365.

touchstone by the courts, it will mechanically disclose the truth. I do suggest and believe that empirical solutions will be saner and sounder if in the background of the empiricism there is the study and the knowledge of what men have thought and written in the anxious search and groping for a co-ordinating principle.

Bills of rights give assurance to the individual of the preservation of his liberty. They do not define the liberty they promise. In the beginnings of constitutional government, the freedom that was uppermost in the minds of men was freedom of the body. The subject was not to be tortured or imprisoned at the mere pleasure of the ruler. There went along with this, or grew from it, a conception of a liberty that was broader than the physical. Liberty became identified with the reign of law. "Freedom of men under government," says Locke,[221] "is to have a standing rule to live by, common to every one of that society and made by the legislative power erected in it." The individual may not be singled out from among his fellows, and made the victim of the shafts of malice. Those who are put over him "are to govern by promulgated established law, not to be varied in particular cases, but to have one rule for rich and poor, for the favorite at court and the countryman at plough."[222]

Up to this, there is no restraint upon the scope or

[221] *Treatises on Civil Government*, book 2, sec. 21.
[222] Locke, *op. cit.*, book ii, sec. 142.

force of law so long as it be law, *i.e.*, so long as it be general or equal, a rule as contrasted with an "extemporary decree." [223] Liberty means more than this, however, as a concept of social science. It has come to mean more, at least in our own system, as a concept of constitutional law. The concept in our constitutional development has undergone a steady and highly significant development. The individual may not only insist that the law which limits him in his activities shall impose like limits upon others in like circumstances. He will also be heard to say that there is a domain of free activity that may not be touched by government or law at all, whether the command be special against him or general against him and others. By express provision of the constitution, he is assured freedom of speech and freedom of conscience or religion. These latter immunities have thus the sanctions of a specific pledge, but they are merely phases of a larger immunity which finds expression in the comprehensive declaration that no one shall be deprived of liberty without due process of law. Such at least appears to be the more recent doctrine of the court that speaks the final word.[224] Apart from any enumerated phase of liberty and beyond it, this declaration gives immunity against "the play and action of purely personal and arbitrary

[223] Locke, *op. cit.*, book ii, secs. 131, 136.

[224] N. Y. *v.* Gitlow, 1925, 268 U.S. 652; Pierce *v.* Society of the Sisters of the Holy Name of Jesus and Mary, 1925, 268 U.S. 510; Whitney *v.* Cal., 1927, 274 U.S. 357; Warren, "The New 'Liberty' under the Fourteenth Amendment," 39 *Harv. L.R.* 431.

power.'' [225] What is personal and arbitrary in mandate and restraint does not gain rationality and coherence because it takes the form of statute. The legislature does not speak with finality as to the measure of its own powers. The final word is for the courts.

Time does not permit, and my aim does not require, that I should catalogue the cases in which statutes have been condemned as founded on no other basis than malice or caprice. A few typical instances will serve to point my meaning. The government may not prohibit the teaching of a foreign language in private schools and colleges.[226] For the same reason, we can safely say, it may not prohibit the teaching in such places of other branches of human learning. It may not take unto itself exclusively the instruction of the young and mould their minds to its own model by forbidding them to be taught in any schools except its own.[227] Restraints such as these are encroachments upon the free development of personality in a society that is organized on the basis of the family. We reach the penetralia of liberty when we throttle the mental life of a group so fundamental.[228] On a plane less exalted than these decisions that deal with the liberty of the spirit are those that limit the power of government in the field of economic liberty. The

[225] Yick Wu *v.* Hopkins, 1886, 118 U.S. 35, 369.
[226] Meyer *v.* Nebraska, 1923, 262 U.S. 390; Bartels *v.* Iowa, 1923, 262 U.S. 404.
[227] Pierce *v.* Society, etc., 1925, 268 U.S. 510.
[228] *Cf.* Spinoza, *Tractatus Politicus*, ch. 8.

legislature may not require the payment to women
workers of a minimum wage, though the wage does
not exceed what is essential for the needs of decent
living; [229] it may not prohibit employers from dis-
criminating against employes who are connected
with a labor union; [230] it may not abolish the equitable remedy of an injunction in controversies between
capital and labor; [231] it may not require the submission of industrial disputes to boards of arbitra-
tion; [232] it may not even regulate the weight of loaves
of bread,[233] nor forbid the introduction of shoddy
into mattresses.[234]

I have no purpose at this time to debate the much-
debated question whether these cases or some of
them might better have been decided differently. As
to that the court has spoken with an authority all its
own. My purpose is merely to inquire whether liberty
may not have a meaning as a concept of social science
which will have illumination for problems of this order as they come before the court hereafter. The
search is for some co-ordinating principle, whether
the principle be rooted in history or in philosophy,
in a study of what has been or in some effort of pure
reason to determine what ought to be. I shall leave it

[229] Adkins *v.* Children's Hospital, 1923, 261 U.S. 525.
[230] Coppage *v.* Kansas, 1915, 236 U.S. 1.
[231] Truax *v.* Corrigan, 1921, 257 U.S. 312.
[232] Wolff Packing Co. *v.* Industrial Court, 1922, 262 U.S. 522; and, 267 U.S. 552.
[233] Burns Baking Co. *v.* Bryan, 1923, 264 U.S. 504.
[234] Weaver *v.* Palmer Bros. Co., 1926, 270 U.S. 402.

to others to apply the pronouncements of social science to the specific cases I have mentioned. It would not detract from the importance of the inquiry though it were found that in some instances, or even in many, the application would yield results at variance with those accepted by the court. I am concerned with a method that may have value in the future. I may seem to quote overmuch. My excuse is the desire to make manifest the truth that back of what I write is the sanction of something stronger than my own unaided thought.

IV

Liberty and Government — Conclusion

History and reason unite in the warning that "liberty" is impaired by statutes clogging or diverting the free development of personality, or, in other words, of mind or spirit. By history, I have in mind specifically our own history, our own institutional origins; by reason, the scientific interpretation of the ideal of social welfare in the light of universal history, psychology and ethics. Our own institutional origins give the angle of departure. "I have sworn upon the altar of the living God eternal hostility against every form of tyranny over the mind of man." The words are those of Jefferson, but the spirit was in the air. In that faith was organized what Professor Beard has called the great American tradition.[235] To the minds of the fathers of the nation repression of thought and speech, and above all repression of conscience, were vivid and portentous evils.[236] Liberty in its other phases was guaranteed

[235] Beard, "The Great American Tradition," *The Nation*, vol. 123, no. 3183, p. 7, July 7, 1926; *cf.*, Beard, *The Rise of American Civilization*, vol. 1, pp. 151, 152, 160, 185, 379, 449, 487.

[236] See *e.g.*, Jefferson's *Bill for the Introduction of Religious Freedom in Virginia*; also his notes on Virginia, quoted by Hirst, *Life and Letters of Thomas Jefferson*, pp. 136, 138; Franklin, and

in generalities that were pregnant with uncertainty. The deliverance of the soul was proclaimed in the forefront of our bill of rights, where all might know it as a cornerstone of our political philosophy. Some doubtless there were even in those days who lost their hold upon these verities of the spirit when theory met the test of practice. Witness the Sedition Act of 1798.[237] Yet deeper and more overwhelming than the passing inroad upon principle was the backwash of the returning wave. True, indeed, it is that the tide was to ebb and flow thereafter. The article of the constitution which proclaimed the emancipation of the spirit was not phrased, nor could it be, in terms so definite and certain as to avoid the opportunity for conflicting interpretations when specific measures from time to time were subjected to its test. With all these allowances the underlying principle of our political philosophy — the great American tradition — has been for the life of the mind the principle of liberty. "Ye shall know the truth, and the truth shall make you free."

In unison with the voice of history as it spoke at our national beginnings is the deeper voice of science, the science of social life, interpreting universal history and the fundamental needs of man. Personal

the questions put to new members of his Academy, Beard, *op. cit.*, p. 169; Chafee, *Freedom of Speech in War Time*, pp. 4, 21, 23.

[237] *Cf.* Whipple, *The History of Civil Liberty in the United States*; also address by Judge Irving Lehman on "Religious Liberty in New York," printed in *N.Y.L.J.* of May 6, 1927; Beard, *op. cit.*, p. 543.

liberty is a poor and shrunken thing, incapable of satisfying our aspirations or our wants, if it does not exact as its minimal requirement that there shall be the maintenance of opportunity for the growth of personality.[238] "He is the free man," said Spinoza, "who lives according to the dictates of reason alone." [239] We are free only if we know, and so in proportion to our knowledge. There is no freedom without choice, and there is no choice without knowledge, — or none that is not illusory. Implicit, therefore, in the very notion of liberty is the liberty of the mind to absorb and to beget. Here is the fundamental privilege to be maintained in Lord Acton's words, "against the influence of authority and majorities, customs and opinion." [240] "His one belief," says Dr. Figgis, in summarizing Acton's character, "his one belief was the right of every man not to have but to be his best." [241] The mind is in chains when it is without the opportunity to choose. One may argue, if one please, that opportunity to choose is more an evil than a good. One is guilty of a contradiction if one says that the opportunity can be denied, and liberty subsist. At the root of all liberty is the liberty to know.

This freedom of the soul in some of its major postulates, the freedom to speak and write, had its

238 *Cf.* Hobhouse, *Social Evolution and Political Theory*, p. 199.
239 Spinoza, *Ethics*, p. 187, Everyman's ed., also p. 158.
240 Lord Acton, *The History of Freedom and other Essays*, p. 3.
241 *The History of Freedom and other Essays*, Introduction, p. xxvii.

classic vindication by Milton nearly three centuries
ago.[242] The vindication was aimed at a particular
form of encroachment upon the free development of
mind, but it has implications not to be confined to its
immediate occasion. What is true of restrictions upon printing must be true of other restrictions upon
the movement of ideas. They are all condemned by
the same curse. The difficulty about them is that they
presuppose a gift of prophecy in fields where history
makes it plain that prophecy is futile. Galileo and
Copernicus and Bruno have taught us many lessons,
yet not the least is the lesson of intellectual humility.
"Raised to Giordano Bruno by the generation which
he foresaw," — the inscription that commemorates
his glory and his torment,[243] has disquieting remind-
ers. It tells us that the burning of books, the holo-
caust of ideas, is likely to be as ineffective as the
burning of bodies, and almost as odious for those
who light the fires. Experimentation there may be in
many things of deep concern, but not in setting
boundaries to thought, for thought freely commun-
icated is the indispensable condition of intelligent
experimentation, the one test of its validity.[244] As to
this minimal postulate of liberty, the concord of
opinion among students of the social sciences is un-

[242] *The Areopagitica*, a plea for the liberty of unlicensed printing,
1644.

[243] Robinson, *The Mind in the Making*, p. 219; White, *History of
the Warfare of Science with Theology*, vol. 1, p. 57; *cf.*, MacDonnell, *Historical Trials*, Bruno, pp. 66, 83.

[244] *Cf.* Bury, *A History of Freedom of Thought*, pp. 233, 239.

broken and impressive. Reason has combined with emotion, thought reacted upon custom, in the up-building of an ethos, after the manner described by Hobhouse in his analysis of the process.[245] ''The struggle of reason against authority,'' says Dr. Bury, summing up his review of the history of the conflict,[246] ''has ended in what appears now to be a decisive and permanent victory for liberty. In the most civilized and progressive countries, freedom of discussion is recognized as a fundamental principle. In fact, we may say it is accepted as a test of en-lightenment, and the man in the street is forward in acknowledging that countries like Russia and Spain, where opinion is more or less fettered, must on that account be considered less civilized than their neigh-bors.'' The man in the street this time has the phil-osopher beside him. If political philosophy has any message to impart, the right of the individual, ''not to have but to be his best,'' has been accredited by the voice of wisdom as an inexpugnable inheritance, the good that it secures one of the accepted treasures of mankind.

We begin with Spinoza whose *Tractatus Theolo-gico-Politicus* was published anonymously in 1670, contemporaneously almost with Milton's plea for liberty. ''The more obstinately freedom of speech has been denied the more resolutely have mankind striven against the restraint, — not flatterers and

[245] *Ante*, p.
[246] *Op. cit.*, p. 247.

sycophants indeed, ... but those whom a liberal education and integrity of life have made more free. ... Men in general are so constituted that they bear nothing more impatiently than to see opinions which they hold for true regarded as crimes, and all that moves them to piety towards God and charity towards man accounted for wickedness; whence it comes that laws are detested, and whatever can be adventured against authority is held to be not base and reprehensible, but brave and praiseworthy. ... They ... are the true disturbers of the state who in a free commonwealth refuse that liberty of opinion which cannot be repressed.'' [247]

Modern speculation in sociology and ethics has been able to do little more than elaborate and fortify this triumphant declaration of the explosive power of mind.

''The value of liberty,'' says Hobhouse,[248] ''is to build up the life of the mind while the value of state control lies in securing the external conditions, including the mutual restraint, whereby the life of the mind is rendered secure. In the former sphere, compulsion only defeats itself. In the latter liberty defeats itself. Hence in the main the extension of control docs not impair liberty, but on the contrary is itself the means of extending liberty and may and should be conceived with that very object in view.

[247] Spinoza, *Tractatus Theologico-Politicus*, translation by Willis, published in London, 1868, pp. 348, 351; Frank Thilly, *Spinoza's Doctrine of the Freedom of Peace*, 1923, pp. 88, 102.
[248] *Social Evolution and Political Theory*, p. 202.

Thus it is that upon the whole we see a tendency to the removal of restraints in the sphere in which whatever there is of value to mankind depends on spontaneity of impulse, free interchange of ideas, and voluntary coöperation going along with the tendency to draw tighter the bonds which restrain men from acting directly or indirectly to the injury of their fellows and to enlarge the borders of the action of the state in response to a developing sense of collective responsibility. We are dealing with two conditions of harmonious development apparently opposed and requiring themselves to be rendered harmonious by careful appreciation of their respective functions, and the general direction in which harmony is to be sought may be expressed by saying that the further development of the state lies in such an extension of public control as makes for the fuller development of the life of the mind.''

The same author recurs to the same theme in another of his books,[249] and develops it acutely.

''There is no true opposition,'' he says, ''between liberty as such and control as such, for every liberty rests on a corresponding act of control. The true opposition is between the control that cramps the personal life and the spiritual order and the control that is aimed at securing the external and material conditions of their free and unimpeded development.'' And again:[250] ''Liberalism applies the wis-

[249] *Liberalism*, p. 147.
[250] P. 118.

dom of Gamaliel in no spirit of indifference, but in the full conviction of the potency of truth. If this thing be of man, *i.e.*, if it is not rooted in actual verity, it will come to nought. If it be of God, let us take care that we be not found fighting against God." [251]

So, Laski, in his *Grammar of Politics*: "What seems to be of the permanent essence of freedom is that the personality of each individual should be so unhampered in its development, whether by authority or by custom, that it can make for itself a satisfactory harmonisation of its impulses." [252] "Where restraint becomes an invasion of liberty is where the given prohibition acts so as to destroy that harmony of impulses which comes when a man knows that he is doing something it is worth while to do. Restraint is felt as evil when it frustrates the life of spiritual enrichment." [253] "The freedoms I must possess to enjoy a general liberty are those which, in their sum, will constitute the path through which my best self is capable of attainment. That is not to say it will be attained. It is to say only that I alone can make that best self, and that without those freedoms I have not the means of manufacture at my disposal." [254] "Freedoms are therefore opportunities which history has shown to be essential to the development of personality." [255]

[251] *Cf.* Maitland, *Collected Papers*, Liberty, vol. 3, p. 90.
[252] P. 102.
[253] P. 143.
[254] P. 144.
[255] P. 144; *cf.* Dewey, *The Public and its Problems*, p. 150.

Quotation may close with the words of a great apostle of liberty who foresaw that his plea for the free development of the spirit would be likely to survive when his other contributions to our knowledge of the life of the mind should be distanced in the march of thought.

"If all mankind," says Mill in his essay on *Liberty*,[256] "if all mankind minus one were of one opinion and only one person were of the contrary opinion, mankind would be no more justified in silencing that person than he, if he had the power, would be justified in silencing mankind. Were an opinion a personal possession of no value except to the owner; if to be obstructed in the enjoyment of it were simply a private injury, it would make some difference whether the injury was inflicted only on a few persons or on many. But the peculiar evil of silencing the expression of an opinion is, that it is robbing the human race; posterity as well as the existing generation; those who dissent from the opinion still more than those who hold it. If the opinion is right, they are deprived of the opportunity of exchanging error for truth; if wrong, they lose, what is almost as great a benefit, the clearer perception and livelier impression of truth, produced by its collision with error."[257]

The acceptance of this principle, like that of any other so general or abstract, does not mean, of

[256] P. 79, Everyman's ed.
[257] *Cf.* MacIver, *The Modern State*, p. 153.

course, that application to particular cases is without the opportunity for error. What Stammler says of the process of subsumption is true here as elsewhere. "So far," he says,[258] "as there are still doubts remaining in carrying out the method of just law, this is due to the problem of subsumption generally. For the subordination of a particular case to a general proposition can never be carried out with absolute precision. For there is no mathematical basis on the one hand, and on the other hand, there are other things at stake than the mere logical arrangement of concepts."[259] The right of free development does not exclude the right of government to insure for the young a minimum of knowledge. There is, of course, an opportunity even here for illegitimate encroachment. The state under the guise of paternal supervision may attempt covertly and gradually to mould its members to its will. The difference as so often is a difference of degree. The world has a certain stock of knowledge which has been garnered through the toil of centuries. The value of this stock has been so tested and verified by successive generations that to shut the young out from the opportunity of sharing in it would be to shut them out from the opportunity of pushing the bounds of knowledge farther. If private schools do not reach a level of reasonable competence, the state may insist that the young shall be trained in its own schools till this level is attained.

258 *Op. cit.*, p. 233.
259 See also *op. cit.*, p. 239.

That is a very different exercise of power from the suppression of private schools altogether, irrespective of their merit, in furtherance of a purpose to give to all within the state a cast and mode of thought established by itself. We may ask how we are to know when the required level has been reached. There is no other standard save the judgment of the elect, the judgment of skill and experience, the judgment of those trained in pedagogics. To this the courts will refer, and by this, when ascertained, they will be bound, though the function of ascertaining it will, of course, be theirs. Like difficulties may be encountered in precincts not judicial, as, for example, in the universities with their ever recurring problem of academic freedom. There is general agreement that a teacher is not to be dismissed unless for some better reason than the fact that he has inculcated novel or heterodox or unpopular doctrine, yet novelty or heterodoxy or unpopularity may be so extreme as to be other names for ignorance. The stream of principle will seem to lose itself at times in all the maze of varying circumstance, yet it emerges in the end and pursues its shining course.

Troublesome, too, at times are the distinctions between thought and conduct. The liberty that is assured to us is not liberty to act. It is liberty to think and speak. Thought and speech in certain contexts may be equivalent to acts. When this boundary is reached, we reach the limit of immunity. ''No one

pretends," says Mill,[260] "that acts should be as free
as opinions. On the contrary, even opinions lose their
immunity where the circumstances in which they are
expressed are such as to constitute their expression
a positive instigation to some mischievous act. An
opinion that corn-dealers are starvers of the poor, or
that private property is robbery, ought to be unmo-
lested when simply circulated through the press, but
may justly incur punishment when delivered orally
to an excited mob assembled before the house of a
corn-dealer, or when handed about among the same
mob in the form of a placard. Acts, of whatever kind,
which, without justifiable cause, do harm to others
may be, and in the more important cases, absolutely
require to be, controlled by unfavorable sentiments,
and, when needful by the active interference of mankind." [261] So Hobhouse: [262] "Even in regard to matter of opinion it is only opinion and persuasion that
can be absolutely free, and even here it must be admitted that there are forms of persuasion that are
in fact coercive, and it is fair for the state to consider how far the liberty of the younger or weaker
must be protected against forms of temptation which
overcome the will. Apart from this when opinion
leads, however conscientiously, to action, such action

260 *Liberty*, Everyman's ed., p. 114.

261 "The most stringent protection of free speech would not pro-
tect a man in falsely shouting fire in a theatre and causing a panic."
— Holmes, J., in Scheneck *v.* U. S., 1916, 249 U.S. 47, 52.

262 *Social Evolution and Political Theory*, p. 200; *cf.* the same author's *Liberalism*, p. 148.

may coerce others, and this would bring the state into play in the name of liberty itself.''[263]

One will find it instructive to apply these pronouncements to some of the rulings of the courts. We may apply them, *e.g.*, to the ruling that the institution of polygamy is not protected by the constitution against abolition by the legislature because the supposed virtue of the practice is a tenet of a church.[264] We may apply them again to limitations upon freedom of utterance that have been held to be permissible in the emergency of war, or, for the preservation of the state, in times of peace as well. Here restraint and immunity have troublesome gradations. ''There may indeed be breaches of the peace,'' says Stephen in his *History of the Criminal Law*,[265] which may destroy or endanger life, limb or property, and there may be incitements to such offenses. But no imaginable censure of the government, short of a censure which has an immediate tendency to produce such a breach of the peace, ought to be regarded as criminal.''[266] We may say the same of expressions of opinion generally. Yet the test is one that it is easier to state than to apply. There are rulings in recent cases as, *e.g.*, in Abrams *v.* U. S., 1919, 250 U.S. 616, and N. Y. *v.* Gitlow, 1925, 268 U.S. 652,

[263] See the same author's *Liberalism*, p. 148, and his *Elements of Social Justice*, pp. 73, 74; but *cf.* Laski, *A Grammar of Politics*, p. 120, and the same author's *Authority in the Modern State*, p. 56.

[264] Reynolds *v.* U. S., 1878, 98 U.S. 145.

[265] Vol. 2, p. 300.

[266] See also Holdsworth, *History of English Law*, vol. 8, p. 338.

that have provoked a sharp division of opinion among the judges of our highest court.[267] The division is a warning that delicate must be the scales for the weighing of the interactions between behavior and belief. If the reading of the balance is doubtful, the presumption in favor of liberty should serve to tilt the beam. That lesson, if no other, stands out from the surrounding darkness. Aglow even yet, after the cooling time of a century and more, is the coal from the fire that was the mind of Voltaire: ''I do not believe in a word that you say, but I will defend to the death your right to say it.''

When we pass from liberty of mind or spirit to other forms of liberty, and particularly economic liberty, we are in the grip of other troubles. The problem may not be more delicate, but at least it is more intricate, less unified and isolated. Especially is this so when we view it as a legal rather than a social problem, for our constitutional law in its development of the idea of liberty may not press development so far as to trench upon an institution constitutionally protected, the institution of private property. Statutes may go down because impairing an essential incident of property, though by establishing a wider distribution of equality they might tend to economic liberty. The teachings of the social scientist must be corrected so as to make allowance for these deflecting forces before applying them to

[267] *Cf.* Brandeis, J., in Whitney *v.* Cal., 1927, 274 U.S. 357, 372.

law. This does not mean, however, that they are to
be neglected altogether.

I find no clearer exposition of the trend of social
thought in the domain of economic liberty than in
Hobhouse's book on *Liberalism*, the chapter on
"Laissez faire." At the outset, the Manchester
school opposed the regulation of hours of labor for
industrial workmen through governmental action.
Regulation was thought to be inconsistent with liberty of contract. Before long the truth became evi-
dent that the liberty was verbal only. "Here was
the owner of a mill employing five hundred hands.
Here was an operative possessed of no alternative
means of subsistence seeking employment. Suppose
them to bargain as to terms. If the bargain failed,
the employer lost one man and had four hundred
and ninety-nine to keep his mill going. At worst, he
might for a day or two, until another operative appeared, have a little difficulty in working a single
machine. During the same days the operative might
have nothing to eat and might see his children hun-
gry. Where was the effective liberty in such an arrangement?" [268] Trade unionism developed in an
effort to adjust the balance. The benefit that came
thereby to workmen enforced an important lesson of
far wider application. This was that "in the matter
of contract true freedom postulates substantial
equality between the parties. In proportion as one
party is in a position of vantage, he is able to dictate

[268] Hobhouse, *op. cit.*, pp. 83, 84.

his terms. In proportion as the other party is in a weak position, he must accept unfavorable terms." [269]

De Tocqueville was impressed with the belief that the love of equality is stronger in most minds than the love of liberty. But the opposition is unreal. Equality is the necessary condition of liberty, or at any rate of social liberty as contrasted with liberty that is unsocial or anarchical. At the root of the preference of equality, there is thus a sound core of intuition. "Liberty without equality is a name of noble sound and squalid result." [270]

The perception of this truth has brought about a growing acceptance in our law of the power of the legislature to regulate industrial conditions — to establish some degree of equality of opportunity between the affluent and the needy. There was opposition to the movement, based upon an individualistic philosophy which permeated for a time the decisions of the courts, yet the movement gained an impetus that could not be withstood. We find, accordingly, that there may be legislation requiring the use of safety devices in tenements and factories; invalidating contracts whereby the workmen release the master from his statutory duty; limiting the hours of work for women, and at last, after much hesitation, the hours of work for men. England has established wages boards in "sweated industries" which fix wages paid to workers without limitation of age or

[269] *Ibid.*, p. 85.
[270] Hobhouse, *Liberalism*, p. 86.

sex.[271] A decision of our Supreme Court has drawn a distinction between regulation of hours and regulation of wages.[272] There surely is none when liberty is viewed, not negatively or selfishly as a mere absence of restraint, but positively and socially as an adjustment of restraints to the end of freedom of opportunity. The decision evoked sharp dissent among the members of the court and animated criticism by leaders of juristic thought.[273]

I have said that the answer of social science is not doubtful when met by problems of this order. "There emerges," says Hobhouse,[274] "a distinction between social and unsocial freedom. Unsocial freedom is the right of a man to use his powers without regard to the wishes and interests of any one except himself. Such freedom is theoretically possible for an individual. It is antithetic to all public control. It is theoretically impossible for a plurality of individuals living in mutual contact. Socially it is a contradiction unless the desires of all men were automatically attuned to social ends. Such freedom, then, for any epoch short of the millenium rests on restraint. It is a freedom that can be enjoyed by all the members of a community, and it is the freedom to choose among those lines of activity which do not involve injury to others. As experience of the social

271 Hobhouse, *Liberalism*, p. 86.

272 Adkins *v.* Children's Hospital, 1923, 261 U.S. 525.

273 See the volume *The Supreme Court and Minimum Wage Legislation*, published by *New Republic, Inc.*, New York, 1925.

274 *Liberalism*, p. 91.

effects of action ripens and as the social conscience is awakened, the conception of injury is widened and insight into its causes is deepened. The area of restraint is therefore increased.''

''It might seem to the superficial observer,'' writes a thoughtful student of the social structure,[275] ''as if the increase of control, inspection, regulation, under democracy meant a greater abrogation of personality. But it is necessary to weigh liberty against liberty, and then we see that on the whole (whatever criticisms and exceptions we may make) the newer restrictions on liberty are incidental, leaving the essential individuality free, as contrasted with the older restrictions which struck at the very heart of individuality.''

I come back to the words of Hobhouse: ''As experience of the social effects of action ripens and as the social conscience is awakened, the conception of injury is widened, and insight into its causes is deepened. The area of restraint is therefore increased.'' We must learn the lesson that the freedoms comprehended within the concept ''liberty'' are not the same at different places or at different epochs. Restrictions necessary in a dense and highly organized industrial community may be arbitrary and oppressive in a pioneer community of agriculturists or miners. The physical and geographical conditions, mountains, crops and weather, affect the manner of life, and so the rules and liberties of life.[276] Economic

[275] MacIver, *Community*, p. 317.
[276] Barnes, *Sociology and Political Theory*, pp. 30, 66.

conditions have, of course, a potency not easily obscured. Our statutes against monopoly and against combinations in restraint of trade bear witness to the underlying assumption of our law that liberty can be pushed to a point at which liberty is destroyed. The lesson, of course, is that in fixing the content of the constitutional immunity, we must test the validity of statutes with our eyes ever on the concrete fact. We must know how men work, and how they live, before we can say whether liberty will be increased or diminished by regulations affecting the manner of their living.

With all this knowledge gained, there will be chance enough for error. We shall have before us still "the everlasting enigma in law and life: when is far too far?" [277] Yet there are signposts on the way, if only we have skill to read them. Lord Acton tells us that "the example of the Hebrew nation laid down the parallel lines on which all freedom has been won, the doctrine of national tradition and the doctrine of the higher law; the principle that a constitution grows from a root by a process of development, and not of essential change; and the principle that all political authority must be tested and reformed according to a code which was not made by man." [278] To the test of these doctrines the concrete facts must be subjected, after they have been labor-

[277] Frankfurter and Corcoran, "Petty Offences and Trial by Jury," 39 *Harvard L.R.* 981.

[278] Acton, *History of Freedom and other Essays*, "Freedom in Antiquity," p. 5.

iously gathered, before we shall be able to interpret their significance. The doctrine of traditional development will forbid far-reaching change, change revolutionary in the suddenness of its onset and the extent of its upheaval. Yet the censor will have need of caution and humility. In a representative democracy, the occasions will be rare indeed when a cataclysmic rupture of the existing legal order will have the approval of a legislature chosen from the body of the people. "Historic continuity in constitutional construction" it has been said, "does not necessarily mean historic stereotype in application. To what extent respect for continuity demands adherence merely to what was, involves the art of adjudication — raises those questions of more or less that ultimately decide cases."[279] Legislature as well as court is an interpreter and a guardian of constitutional immunities.[280] We are to beware of the insularity of mind that perceives in every inroad upon habit a catastrophic revolution. There remains, however, a second test. The doctrine of the higher law, which today has no theological implications, or none that are necessarily theological, but is rather Stammler's doctrine of a natural law with a changing content [281] — the doctrine of the higher law will test the validity

[279] Frankfurter and Corcoran, ''Petty Federal Offences and Trial by Jury,'' 39 *H.L.R.* 922.

[280] M. K. & T. Ry. Co. *v.* May, 1904, 194 U.S. 267, 270; People *v.* Crane, 1915, 214 N.Y. 154, 173.

[281] See Cardozo, *Nature of the Judicial Process*, p. 132; also Laski, *English Political Theory*, Home University Library, p. 60; Charmont,

of change within the limits of national tradition by its tendency to advance or retard the free development of personality in the conditions of time and place prevailing when the change is made.

There is a modern doctrine of natural rights which retains the label, but only in a slight degree the content, of the doctrine of natural rights as it was developed a century and more ago. You will find the present view-point conveniently and clearly summarized in a little book, *The Ethical Basis of the Modern State*, by Professor Norman Wilde of the University of Minnesota. "The modern doctrine of natural rights is realistic and historic. It knows nothing of humanity as such and its abstract rights, but finds only a varying body of traditions as to what are the essential conditions of social welfare. At every stage in the development of a people are found certain standards of living that fix the terms upon which men are willing to endure a given order. As long as society meets these terms they are willing to go peaceably about their business, but if these terms are not met and their fundamental habits of living and acting are interfered with, they rebel and demand their rights. What these fundamental rights are is not determined by human nature in the abstract, but by the custom and expectations of a given age and people. We may speak vaguely of life, liberty, and the pursuit of property and happiness, but

La Renaissance du Droit Naturel, 7 Modern Legal Phil.Series, p. 111; Borchard, "Government Responsibility in Tort," 36 *Yale Law Journal.*

these moving terms have no meaning save as interpreted as terms of particular men and times. In every growing society there is as much need for the revision and reinterpretation of its rights as there is in the growing child for the alteration of its clothes.'' [282]

The guaranty of liberty in the constitutional law of the nation and its constituent commonwealths is a guaranty that claims and immunities conceived of at any given stage of civilization as primary and basic shall be preserved against destruction or encroachment by the agencies of government. We may classify under this head some of the decisions defining those indispensable elements of justice that are essential to the attainment of due process of law. There must be judgment after notice and a hearing. There must be trial by an impartial judge without interest in the event. Only the other day this principle was held to invalidate a conviction by a justice of the peace whose fees were proportioned to the fines that he imposed.[283] There must be calmness and deliberation, or at least the fair opportunity for them. A trial is none in substance, whatever it may be in form, if the verdict does no more than register the bidding of a mob.[284] Here are illustrations of possible encroachments upon the precincts of a freedom

[282] Wilde, *The Ethical Basis of the State*, p. 83; *cf.* M. R. Cohen, ''Jus Naturale Redivivum,'' 25 *Phil. Rev.* 761; Laski, *Authority in the Modern State*, pp. 64, 65.

[283] Tumey *v.* Ohio, 1927, 273 U.S. 510.

[284] Moore *v.* Dempsey, 1923, 261 U.S. 86.

that is primary and basic. Encroachments have been adjudged at times when the inroad was less apparent to the eye of philosophy or justice. In particular this has been so in defining the bounds of liberty of contract. The duty of delimiting the sphere of exemption must be cast, however, upon some one. In our constitutional system it has been cast upon the courts. The power is not to be cheapened and made odious by trivial or hasty exercise. It is to be reserved for true emergencies. The urge of selfish groups, or more rarely passion or indifference, may drive the lawmaker at times to forgetfulness or disregard of interests more permanent and essential than those exalted by his statute. It is the theory of our polity that beneath the transitory flux the judge may be expected to discern the deeper principle, and to rescue it from submergence in what is passing and particular.

This conception of liberty and in particular of economic liberty as something fluid and inconstant implies a duty of the courts to look to time and place and circumstance in determining its content. In our day there has been much emphasis of the need that fact finding agencies be organized to the end that time and place and circumstance be exhibited as they are. The complexities of modern life are so great that in the absence of fuller information than is commonly available to judges, the significance of apparent limitations upon liberty is likely to be lost. The result is the treatment of liberty as something

static and predetermined. The decision of the Supreme Court in the Chastleton case [285] may prove to
be the entering wedge that will open up a new technique. The question was whether in the District of
Columbia there had come an end to the emergency
that had been thought to justify a statute limiting
the rents of dwellings. The court said that if its own
judicial knowledge were to be the sole basis of its
action, it would hold that the emergency had passed.
It refused, however, to be so limited, but remitted
the case to the trial court to investigate and report.
There is little doubt that according to the practice in
vogue in many jurisdictions, the court would have
dealt with the case upon the footing of judicial notice. We have here the germ of a method capable of
expansion. Courts should feel freer than they have
hitherto felt to inform their judgment by inquiry.
On the other hand, the very need for such inquiry is
warning that in default of full disclosure of the facts,
there should be submission, readier than has sometimes been accorded, to the judgment of the lawmakers. The presumption of validity should be more
than a pious formula, to be sanctimoniously repeated
at the opening of an opinion and forgotten at the end.

Often a liberal antidote of experience supplies a
sovereign cure for a paralyzing abstraction built
upon a theory. Many a statutory innovation that
would seem of sinister or destructive aspect if it
were considered in advance, has lost its terror with

[285] Chastleton Corporation *v.* Sinclair, 1924, 264 U.S. 543.

its novelty. Take such a group of statutes as the zoning laws that have made their way to recognition and enforcement in so many of our states.[286] I have little doubt that a generation ago they would have been thrown out by the courts as illegitimate encroachments upon that freedom of use which is an attribute of property. I venture to express some doubt as to the fate they would have suffered even in our own day if they had come before the Supreme Court while they were yet novelties in legislation. The fact is, however, that by the time they were subjected to that challenge, they were in successful operation far and wide throughout the land. The test of experience had proved them to be forces that made for conservation rather than destruction. More than that, the values thus maintained were not merely personal or moral — the values of health and comfort and decency and order — though very likely these alone would have sufficed; they were property values too, and thus closely linked to the conservative tradition. The legislation that maintained them might be socialistic in its tendency, but upholders of the existing order could take comfort in the thought that it was neither proletarian nor radical. The ogre lost his talons and assumed the aspect of a friend.

If reasoning is vitiated at times by adhering to abstractions, it is vitiated also by starting with a prepossession and finding arguments to sustain it.

[286] Village of Euclid *v.* Ambler Realty Co., 1926, 272 U.S. 365.

The weakness is inherent in the judicial process.[287] The important thing, however, is to rid our prepossessions, so far as may be, of what is merely individual or personal, to detach them in a measure from ourselves, to build them, not upon instinctive or intuitive likes and dislikes, but upon an informed and liberal culture, a knowledge (as Arnold would have said) of the best that has been thought and said in the world, so far as that best has relation to the social problem to be solved. Of course, when our utmost effort has been put forth, we shall be far from freeing ourselves from the empire of inarticulate emotion, of beliefs so ingrained and inveterate as to be a portion of our very nature. "I must paint what I see in front of me," said the elder Yeats to his son, the poet. "Of course, I shall really paint something different because my own nature will come in unconsciously." [288] There is nothing new in all this. The same lesson was taught us long ago by Bacon in his searching analysis of the idols of the mind. "The human mind resembles those uneven mirrors which impart their own properties to different objects . . . and distort and disfigure them." [289] Yet the lesson, if not new, is also not outworn. Our modern students of the processes of mind and of society do well to place it in the forefront of their teaching. "Psychol-

[287] Laski, *A Grammar of Politics*, p. 544; and *cf.* Laski, "Judicial Review of Social Policy in England," 39 *Harv. L.R.* 832.

[288] W. B. Yeats, *Autobiographies*, p. 101.

[289] *Nov. Org.*, 1, 41.

ogy," says J. A. Hobson,[290] "has almost wiped out
hypocrisy. Sincerity is a matter of degree." The
weakness is not peculiar to reasoning in law; it
extends to reasoning in all the social sciences, and in
some degree to reasoning everywhere. In the words
of Dewey, "Thoughts sprout and vegetate; ideas
proliferate. They come from deep unconscious
sources. . . . The stuff of belief is not originated by
us. It comes to us from others, by education, tradition and the suggestions of the environment." [291] The
best that we can hope for is that from the knowledge
of our weakness there will come the exercise of
strength.

I have said that in our constitutional law, the concept of liberty as formulated by social science must
be so restrained and regulated that there shall be no
undue impairment of rights of private property.
When impairment becomes undue, cannot easily be
stated within the limits of a formula. Again there is
the need for compromise; a median line is to be
drawn between excesses, between an egoism too narrow to be endured and an altruism too broad to be
attained. A like antithesis confronts us in morals as
in law. "It would . . . be a contradictory state of
things," writes Windelband in his *Introduction to
Philosophy*,[292] "if the happiness of the individual
were a value that all others had to respect, yet he

[290] *Free Thought in the Social Sciences*, p. 45.
[291] Dewey, *Human Nature and Conduct*, p. 314; *cf.* Robinson, *The
Mind in the Making*, pp. 59, 60.
[292] P. 226.

himself were forbidden to cultivate it." The institution of private property is the tribute that is paid by law to what is self-regarding in the mind of man. Human nature, however, is not selfishness alone. Judges and lawmakers have seen that private property, if it is to be moulded in response to human needs, must be the expression of an egoism that is shorn of brutality. Some play must be allowed for those altrustic impulses that in any given time and place are habitual and normal. The bundle of power and privileges to which we give the name of ownership is not constant through the ages. The faggots must be put together and rebound from time to time. As I have pointed out before, "Men are saying today that property like every other social institution has a social function to fulfill. Legislation which destroys the institution is one thing. Legislation which holds it true to its function is quite another." [293]

Back of the pronouncements of the courts, one finds a recognition of this truth, though at times there has been too great an emphasis upon the forms of restraint inherited from the past and a corresponding unwillingness to give heed to the necessities of the present. The social urge, even when mak-

[293] Cardozo, *The Nature of the Judicial Process*, p. 87; *cf.* Duguit, *Transformations Generales du Droit Privé Depuis le Code Napoléon*, Continental Legal History Series, vol. xi, p. 74; M. R. Cohen, "Recent Philosophical Legal Literature," *The International Journal of Ethics*, July, 1916, p. 530; also the group of articles on "Property" in the volume of the *Rational Basis of Legal Institutions* in the Modern Legal Philosophy Series, p. 167, *et seq.*

ing itself felt, has been covered and at times obscured under incomplete or question-begging formulas and phrases. The usual statement is that property rights may be limited whenever property is so
circumstanced as to be "affected with a public
use."[294] Under cover of that text, with its convenient, if deceptive, vagueness,[295] many a lesson of
humility has been taught unto the pride of ownership. One business after another has been annexed,
so to speak, to the public domain, which seemed at
times to be capable of indefinite aggrandizement, until only the other day there came an unexpected
check. The decision in the New York Theatre Ticket
Brokers case,[296] rendered by a closely divided court,
has set up a new breakwater in the form of a more
rigid adherence to those restraints and those only
that have become consecrated by the hand of time.
In the meanwhile, however, the surveyor, marking
the contour of the shore, will have set down in his
note book many a change of line. There may be regulation of rates for the use of grain elevators, for
transportation by sea and land, for the use of gas
and water, for telegraphs and telephones, and even
for insurance against fire.[297] Not only that, but a
business strictly private in one set of conditions,
may through other and new conditions become quasi-

[294] Munn v. Illinois, 94 U.S. 113.
[295] Stone, J., dissenting in the New York theatre brokers case, Tyson & Bro. v. Banton, 1927, 273 U.S. 418, 451.
[296] *Supra.*
[297] German Alliance Ins. Co. v. Kansas, 1914, 233 U.S. 389.

public overnight. The owner of land and buildings
may find himself restricted in the rent that he is free
to charge if the emergency is pressing enough to
make the restriction necessary as a means to social
justice.[298] At such times, no antecedent contract will
be permitted to stand in the way of the power of the
state to promote the welfare of its citizens by pro-
tecting them against the encroachments of a rapaci-
ous individualism.[299] The zoning laws have gone still
farther and have extended regulation to property
held for private uses though emergency is absent.
The national government, too, has felt the leash re-
laxed when the necessity was adequate. Congress in
times of stress and strain may take to itself the power of fixing the wages of engineers and others upon
interstate lines of transportation.[300] Even in times
more placid, the railroads may have to submit to the
recaption by the government of a share of their
earnings beyond a maximum percentage.[301] Property,
like liberty, has been taught that some of its most
cherished immunities are not absolute, but relative.
We shall have to learn as the years go by to distinguish more and more between what is essential in the
concept of ownership and so invariable under the

[298] Marcus Brown Holding Co. *v.* Feldman, 1921, 256 U.S. 170;
Block *v.* Hirsch, 1921, 256 U.S. 135; Levy Leasing Co. *v.* Siegel, 1922,
258 U.S. 242; Peo. *ex rel.* Durham Realty Co. *v.* La Fetra, 1921,
230 N.Y. 429.

[299] Levy Leasing Co. *v.* Siegel, *supra*; Union Dry Goods Co. *v.*
Georgia Public Serv. Corp., 1919, 248 U.S. 372.

[300] Wilson *v.* New, 1917, 243 U.S. 332.

[301] Dayton Goose Creek Ry. Co. *v.* U.S., 1924, 263 U.S. 456.

constitution, and what is accidental or unessential, and so variable and severable at the call of social needs.

When we speak of law and liberty and the need of compromise between them, what is uppermost in our minds is commonly the kind of problem that is involved in the definition of the constitutional immunity. In essence, however, the problem is not different whenever a rule of law is extended into fields unoccupied before. "Shall A. answer to B. for the consequences of an act?" means this and nothing more, "Shall the freedom of A. to work damage to B. be restrained so as to preserve to B. the freedom to be exempt from damage?" In determining whether it shall, we must again evaluate the social interests concerned. We have regard to the social interest of certainty. The force of precedent and analogy may lead us to refuse an extension that we would otherwise concede. If these guides are silent or inconclusive, we give heed to the prompting of justice or of expediency, which may shade down from considerations of supreme importance to those of mere convenience. "Das Recht," as Binding puts it, "ist eine Ordnung menschlicher Freiheit." [302] The opposites, liberty and restraint, the individual and the group, are phases of those wider opposites, the one and the many, rest and motion, at the heart of all being. Dichotomy is everywhere.

One of the marks by which we recognize a social

[302] *Cf.* Korkunov, *General Theory of Law*, p. 61.

interest as worthy of protection is the spontaneity
and persistence with which groups are established
to conserve it.[303] The mark, of course, is not infalli-
ble. There are groups, spontaneous and persistent
enough, — camorras, secret orders, revolutionary
bands — whose aims are anti-social. Even so, spontaneity and persistence are tokens not to be ignored
that the associative process is moving toward a
social end. A striking instance of this truth is seen
in the history of trade-unions. At first the law held
them anathema. They were combinations in restraint
of trade, pernicious, it was thought, in so far as they
were effective, and, in the long run, as futile as they
were pernicious, since economic "laws," then supposed to be inexorable, would nullify the gains of
victory, and restore the pre-existing level.[304] The result belied the prophecy. The urge to associate and
unify was too spontaneous and persistent for any
interdict to stifle it. The courts perceived and yield-
ed.[305] They were helped at times by legislation. In
many jurisdictions, however, they reached the same
result unaided. They gave up denouncing as lawless
and unsocial a form of grouping that appeared and
reappeared in response to a social pressure akin in
steadiness and intensity to the pressure that makes
law. Whether the unions were to be classified as jural
persons was another question of quite subsidiary

[303] *Cf.* MacIver, *The Modern State*, p. 475.
[304] J. A. Hobson, *Free Thought in the Social Sciences*, pp. 88, 89;
Beard, *The Rise of American Civilization*, vol. 2, pp. 236, 237.
[305] For a summary of the decisions see 16 *Ruling Case Law*, 418.

importance. What mattered most was that they were lawful. The state would hold them in check as it would hold in check the individual and even the agencies of government.[306] It would not repudiate or destroy them. In the struggle between liberty and restraint, a new liberty, asserting itself persistently and clamorously in the minds and hearts of men, became a liberty secured by law. Out of the psychical urge there had been born the jural right. The peace of a new compromise had been declared between the warring opposites.

I have already quoted a sentence from Strachey's essay on Pope. I venture to repeat it now in the setting in which he placed it. "Antithesis," he says, "permeates the structure; it permeates the whole conception of his work. Fundamental opposites clash and are reconciled." The innominate authors of our common law method of judging might say the same about their handiwork. Antithesis permeates the structure. Here is the mystery of the legal process, and here also is its lure. These unending paradoxes tease us with the challenge of a riddle, the incitement of the chase. The law, like science generally, if it could be followed to its roots, would take us down beneath the veins and ridges to the unplumbed depths of being, the reality behind the veil. The jurist must not despair because his plummets do not reach the goal at which in vain for two thousand years and more the philosophers have been casting theirs.

[306] Barker, *Political Thought from Spencer to Today*, p. 179.

Rather will he learn with some of the philosophers themselves in moderating his ambitions to recast to some extent his notion of philosophy and to think of it as a means for the truer estimate of values and the better ordering of life.[307] He will hope indeed that with study and reflections there may develop in the end some form of calculus less precarious than any that philosopher or lawyer has yet been able to devise. In the meantime, amid the maze of contingency and regularity, he will content himself as best he can with his little compromises and adjustments, the expedients of the fleeting hour. They will fret him sometimes with a sense of their uncertainty. It should hearten him to keep in mind that uncertainty is the lot of every branch of thought and knowledge when verging on the ultimate. "To whatever domain of intellectual activity you may address your inquiry," I quote the words of a distinguished judge, "you will find in the upper levels of research and judgment grave differences of opinion among the elect few." [308] There is tonic in that thought. There is even greater tonic in the thought that on our side are unseen and masterful allies, who are helping us to win the fight by a power not our own. For the process by which law grows is above all a social process. The individual intellect is not as desolate as it seems. The pressure that gives form to manners and morals

[307] Dewey, *Experience and Nature*, pp. 394, 396, 398, 403, 404, 408; Dewey, *Reconstruction in Philosophy*, pp. 122, 124.

[308] Chas. E. Hughes, address at the Sixtieth Convocation of the University of the State of New York, October 17, 1924.

gives form in the end to law; to judge-made law often, and when on occasion that fails, to law declared by statute. Initiative, ingenuity, idealism will help. For a time the lack of them may deflect and hinder. But the steady pressure goes on, and finds in the end the responsive mind.

Strepsiades in the Greek play was eager to escape the payment of his debts. He was told that the Sophists, led by Socrates, had a good λόγος and a bad one, and that through the bad one injustice could be made to masquerade as justice. So he went expectantly to the school, and prayed to be made perfect in the logic that could cheat. He was old and dull-witted, and could not learn, and his son of quicker wit became the pupil in his stead. The son learned only too well the lesson of the wicked logic. He proved before long to the luckless father that it is the duty of a son to beat his parents and despoil them. So the play ends with Strepsiades disillusioned and repentant. The wicked logic must be abjured; the good one marks the path of happiness and peace.

I have faith with Aristophanes that it is so. Yet even as of old, the rival logics can be heard contending in the law courts of today, and the seeker after peace and happiness is still bewildered by the din.

INDEX

A

Abrams *v.* U. S., 114
Academic freedom, 112
Acton, Lord, 104, 120
Adams *v.* Tanner, 25
Adkins *v.* Children's Hospital, 100, 118
Administrative and judicial functions of judges, 10
Agency, 20-21
Alexander, Archibald, 38
American Bank & Trust Co. *v.* Federal Reserve Bank, 19
American Law Institute, 76
Ames, 19
Andrews, W. S., 5, 25
Aristotle, 28, 38-39, 56
Axiology, 52

B

Bacon, Francis, 127
Baker, 59
Balancing of interests, 67 ff.
Bank of Manhattan Co. *v.* Morgan, 14
Barker, Ernest, 90, 91, 134
Barnes, Harry Elmer, 8, 50, 87, 119
Bartels *v.* Iowa, 99
Beale, Joseph H., 86
Beard, Charles A., 102
Beard, Charles and Mary, 51, 52, 102, 103, 133

Beardsley *v.* Kilmer, 19
Bechuan Land Exploration Co. *v.* London Trading Co., 14
Bentham, 25, 32
Bijur, Mr. Justice, 91
Bills of lading, 12 ff.
Bills of rights, 97, 103
Binding, 132
Bird *v.* Ins. Co., 84, 85
Birkenhead, Lord, 34, 79
Blackstone, 65
Blasphemy, 24-25
Block *v.* Hirsch, 131
Bohlen, F. H., 40, 73, 86
Borchard, E. M., 49, 91, 122
Bouglé, 52, 53, 54, 58
Bowman *v.* The Secular Society, 24
Bowne *v.* Keane, 24
Brandeis, Mr. Justice, 25, 63, 115
Bruno, Giordano, 105
Brütt, 28, 56, 63
Bryce, Lord, 5
Buckley *v.* Mayor, 46
Burns Baking Co. *v.* Bryan, 100
Bury, J. B., 105, 106
Business practice, 15 ff.

C

Cammack *v.* Slattery & Bros., Inc., 71
Campbell *v.* N. Y. Evening Post, 24

Cardozo, B. N., 8, 27, 31, 38, 39, 42, 46, 50, 55, 56, 60, 61, 64, 69, 121, 129
Cause and effect, 81 ff.
Chafee, Z., 103
Change and conservation, 7 ff.
Charmont, 121-122
Chastleton Corporation *v.* Sinclair, 125
Cicero, 51
Cockburn, Lord C. J., 24
Code systems, 28-30
Cohen, M. R., 11, 27, 38, 56, 92, 123, 129
Coleridge, Lord C. J., 26
Compromise, the goal of judicial effort, 5 ff.
Conflict of law, 67
Conservation and change, 7 ff.
Construction of statutes, 9-10
Cooley, 49, 50, 51
Copernicus, 105
Coppage *v.* Kansas, 100
Corporations, 65-66
Crowley *v.* Lewis, 70
Customs, 15 ff

D

Daimler Co. *v.* Continental Tyre Co., 66
Davidson *v.* New Orleans, 96
Davis *v.* Lewis, 23
Dayton Goose Creek Ry. Co. *v.* U. S., 131
Defamation, 22-23
Democracy, 19
Demogue, 5, 6, 36, 39
Depue *v.* Flatau, 40

Dewey, John, 17, 36, 50, 91, 109, 128, 135
Dewey and Tufts, 17, 33, 40
Dickinson, John, 6, 51, 61, 62, 63, 64
Director of Public Prosecutions *v.* Beard, 35
Domestic relations, 18
Duff, P. W., 92
Duguit, 42, 49, 129
Durkheim, E., 53, 54

E

Earl of Northampton's Case, 23
Ecloga, 78
Economic liberty, 115 ff.
Edelstein *v.* Schuler, 14
Edgerton, Henry W., 34-35, 73, 74, 86
Einstein, 11
Equality, 116 ff.
Equilibration of interests, 67
Ethics, 15 ff., 31 ff.
Exchange Bakery *v.* Rifpin, 47

F

Fiction, legal, 33 ff.
Figgis, 104
First National Bank *v.* Carnegie Trust Co., 40
F. L. & T. Co. *v.* Pierson, 91
F. L. & T. Co. *v.* Windthrop, 69
Folkways, 15 ff.
Frankfurter, Felix, 11
Frankfurter and Corcoran, 120, 121
Freedom of speech and of the press, 104 ff.
Freshfield, Edwin Hanson, 78

G

Galileo, 105
Geldart, 91
Geny, François, 27
German Alliance Ins. Co. v. Kansas, 130
Giddings, F. H., 49, 50
Givler, 56
Glasgow Corp. v. Taylor, 46
Goodwin v. Robarts, 14
Government and liberty, 94 ff.
Gray, J. C., 93
Grose, J., 22

H

Haines, 39
Haldane, Lord, 6, 11, 82-83, 84
Halsbury, Lord, 66, 79
Harris v. Shorall, 71
Henderson, G., 91
Herter v. Mullen, 41
Hirst, F. W., 102
Hobhouse, L. T., 16, 17, 36, 38, 49, 50, 51, 89, 95, 96, 104, 106, 107-109, 113-114, 116, 118-119
Hobson, J. A., 128, 133
Hocking, W. E., 36, 49
Holdsworth, W. S., 19, 20, 21, 22, 23, 24, 35, 64, 91, 114
Holmes, O. W., 51, 64, 113
Holt, Lord C. J., 21, 22
Hughes, Charles E., 135
Husband and wife, 18
Hynes v. N. Y. Central R. R. Co., 61

I

Idealism, 27
Individual and society, 86 ff.

In re Debs, 59
Ins. Co. v. Tweed, 85
Interests, balancing of, 67 ff.
Int. Prod. Co. v. Erie R. R. Co., 46

J

James, William, 61
Jaybird Mining Co. v. Weir, 63
Jefferson, Thomas, 102
Jellinek, G., 42
Jhering, 41
Jones, "The Early History of the Fiscus," 92
Judges, administrative and judicial functions of, 10
Justice, precedent and, 29-30; meaning of, 31 ff.

K

Kant, 31, 32, 39
Kaufmann, E., 36
Kerr S. S. Co. v. Radio Corp., 85
Kohler, 83, 91
Korkunov, 17, 42, 132

L

Lalor, 41
Laski, H. J., 49, 88, 91, 109, 114, 121, 123, 127
Law and exact science compared, 1 ff.; problems of, 4 ff.; conflict of, 67
Lefroy, 15, 25, 48
Lehman, Irving, 103
Leibnitz, 80
Leland Shipping Co. v. Norwich Fire Ins. Society, 83
Lévy-Bruhl, 36
Levy Leasing Co. v. Siegel, 131

Liberty, economic, 115 ff.
Liberty and government, 94 ff.
Lippmann, Walter, 12, 50
Locke, John, 94, 97, 98
Lowell, A. L., 50, 51
Lowell, Amy, 60

M

MacDonnell, Sir John, 105
MacIver, R. M., 16, 49, 90, 92, 110, 119, 133
McCarthy v. Henderson, 46
McLaughlin, Chester B., Jr., 12, 13
McLaughlin, James Angell, 86
McPherson v. Daniels, 23
Maitland, F. W., 49, 91, 109
Marcus Brown Holding Co. v. Feldman, 131
Master and servant, 20-21
Matter of Wulfsohn v. Burden, 59
Meyer v. Nebraska, 99
Mill, J. S., 43-45, 110, 112-113
Millar v. Taylor, 15
Milton, John, 105, 106
M. K. & T. Ry. Co. v. May, 121
Moore, George E., 32
Moore v. Dempsey, 123
Morals, 15 ff.; and justice, 31 ff.
Motion, rest and, 7 ff.
Mount Morris Bank v. 23d Ward Bank, 40
Mulleck v. Mulleck, 92
Munn v. Illinois, 130
Myers v. Hurley Motor Co., 46

N

Negligence, 72 ff.

Negotiability, 14
Noble State Bank v. Haskell, 51
N. Y. & B. D. Ex. Co. v. Traders' & M. Ins. Co., 85
N. Y. Theatre Ticket Brokers case, 130
N. Y. v. Gitlow, 98, 114

O

O'Connor v. Hickey, 73
Odgers, 23
Ogburn, W. F., 12
Ogden, 33

P

Pasley v. Freeman, 22
Pearson v. Pearson, 18
Peo. ex rel. Durham Realty Co. v. La Fetra, 131
Peo. ex rel. Wineburgh Adv. Co. v. Murphy, 59
People v. Crane, 121
Perry, R. B., 49, 52
Perry v. Rochester Line Co., 46
Phelps v. Nowlen, 47
Plato, 38
Pierce v. Society of the Sisters of the Holy Name of Jesus and Mary, 98, 99
Ploff v. Putnam, 40
Pollock, Sir Frederick, 10
Pomeroy, J. N., 40
Pompana v. N. Y. Ry. Co., 46
Pound, C. W., 24
Pound, Roscoe, 8, 10, 25, 42, 55, 61
Precedent, 29-30
Press, freedom of the, 104 ff.
Privilege, in libel, 23-24

Progress, stability and, 7 ff.
Property, 115 ff.

Q

Queen *v.* Instan, 25, 26

R

Relativity, 11 ff., 81 ff.
Rest and motion, 7 ff.
Rice *v.* Butler, 46
Rideout *v.* Knox, 47
Robinson, James Harvey, 105, 128
Rogers, A. K., 32
Roguin, E., 93
Rousseau, 88
Royce, Josiah, 57, 62
R. R. Co. *v.* Stout, 46
Russell, Bertrand, 3, 4, 11, 80
R. *v.* Jackson, 18
R. *v.* Ramsay, 24

S

Saint John *v.* Am. Mut. F. & M.
    Ins. Co., 85
Saleilles, R., 93
Salmond, Sir John, 70
Sandburg, Carl, 94
Santayana, George, 79
Scheneck *v.* U. S., 113
Schuyler *v.* Smith, 41
Science, law compared with exact, 1 ff.
Seal, contract under, 70 ff.
Seavey, W. A., 73, 74
Seligman, E. R. A., 90
Sellars, Helen S., 52, 53
Servant, master's liability for contracts and torts of, 20-21
Shaw, Lord, 83

Shearman and Redfield, 46
Slander, 22-23
Small, A. W., 39, 87, 90
Smith, Adam, 33
Society and the individual, 86 ff.
Sorokin, P., 12
Sorrell *v.* Smith, 19
Speech, freedom of, 104 ff.
Spencer, Herbert, 32, 39, 76
Spinoza, 99, 104, 106-107
Stability and progress, 7 ff.
Stammler, Rudolph, 19, 27, 28,
    29, 31, 35-36, 39, 41, 47, 69,
    111, 121
Stare decisis, 8, 64
Statutes, construction of, 9-10
Stephen, Sir James F. J., 114
Stone, Mr. Justice, 130
Strachey, Lytton, 5, 134
Street, T. A., 42
Sumner, Lord, 24
Sumner, William Graham, 16
Superstitious uses, 24-25
Syngenism, 87 ff.

T

Taff Vale Ry. Co. *v.* A. S. R. S.,
    92
Taft, Chief Justice W. H., 51
Taine, H. A., 61
Teaching, freedom in, 111-112
Thilly, Frank, 107
Tocqueville, de, 117
Trade-unions, 133-134
Tradition, 15 ff.
Truax *v.* Corrigan, 100
Tumey *v.* Ohio, 123
Tyson & Bro. *v.* Banton, 130

U

Union Dry Goods Co. *v.* Georgia Public Serv. Corp., 131

United Workers of America *v.* Coronado Coal Co., 92

United Zinc & Capital Co. *v.* Britt, 46

U. P. R. Co. *v.* McDonald, 46

Urban, W. M., 52, 53, 54

Usill *v.* Hales, 23

V

Vaihinger, Hans, 33

Values, science of, 52 ff.

Vietor *v.* National City Bank, 13

Village of Euclid *v.* Ambler Realty Co., 96, 126

Vincent *v.* Lake Erie Transp. Co., 40

Vinogradoff, Sir Paul, 16, 28, 38, 48, 49

Voltaire, 115

W

Wagner *v.* Int. Ry. Co., 73

Wallas, Graham, 60, 61

Walsh *v.* Fitchburgh R. R. Co., 46

Warren, Charles, 98

Wasson *v.* Walter, 24

Weaver *v.* Palmer Bros. Co., 100

Welch *v.* Swasey, 59

Whipple, Leon, 103

White, Andrew D., 105

Whitehead, A. N., 3, 7, 9

Whitney *v.* Cal., 98, 115

Wigmore, J. H., 64

Wilde, Norman, 122-123

Williams *v.* Hays, 73

Willis, Mr. Justice, 15, 107

Williston, Samuel, 71

Wilson *v.* New, 131

Wilson *v.* Walter, 23

Windelband, W., 128-129

Wise, B. R., 93

Wolff Packing Co. *v.* Industrial Court, 100

Wu, John H., 69

Y

Yeats, W. B., 127

Yick Wu *v.* Hopkins, 99

Yome *v.* Gorman, 39

Young, K., 90, 93